TROPHIES

Practice Book

Grade 1 • Volume One

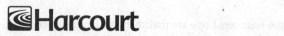

Orlando Boston Dallas Chicago San Diego

Visit *The Learning Site!*
www.harcourtschool.com

Printed in the United States of America

ISBN 0-15-323504-7

25 26 27 28 054 12 11 10 09 08

Contents

GUESS WHO – THEME 1

GUESS WHO – THEME 2

Contents

CATCH A DREAM – THEME 3

Contents

HERE AND THERE – THEME 4

Contents

Name ___

Mm ▶ **Say the name of each picture. If it begins with /m/, write Mm on the lines.**

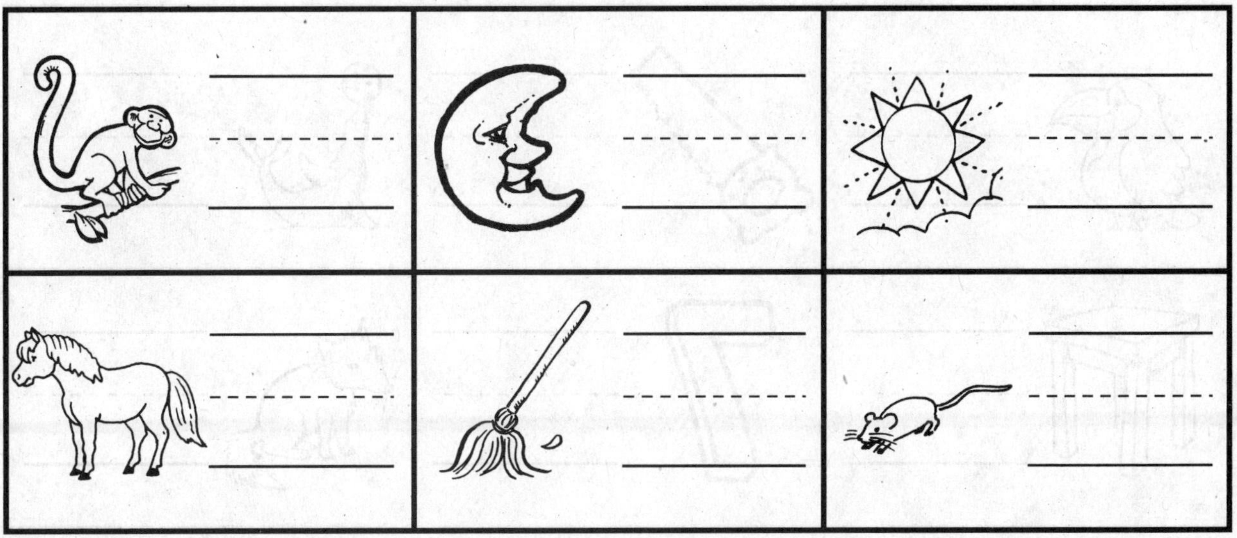

a ▶ **Write a. Draw a picture of something in your classroom. Read.**

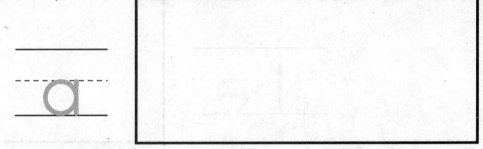

my ▶ **Write my. Draw a picture of something you have. Read.**

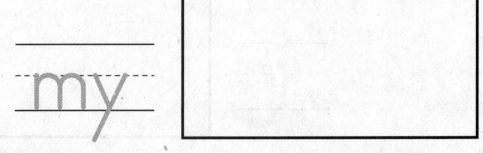

SCHOOL-HOME CONNECTION Ask your child to say each picture name and point to the pictures that begin with the /m/ sound. Have your child practice writing the letters *M* and *m*. Then help your child make up phrases similar to the ones with *a* and *my*.

Name ______________________

Ss ▶ **Say the name of each picture. If it begins with /s/, write Ss on the lines.**

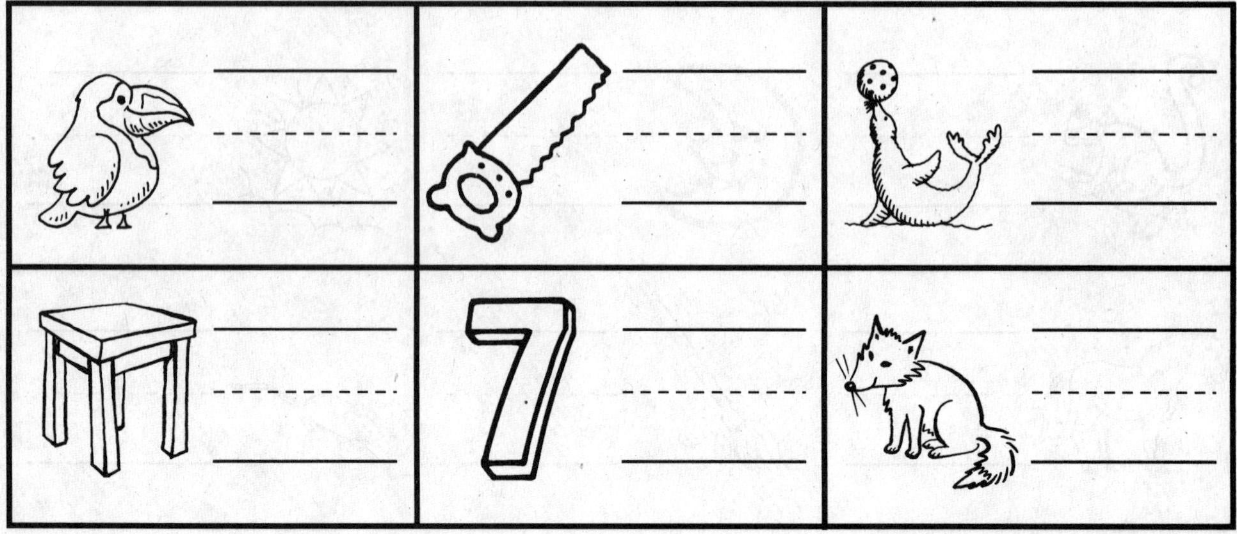

the ▶ **Write the. Draw a picture of something you see. Read.**

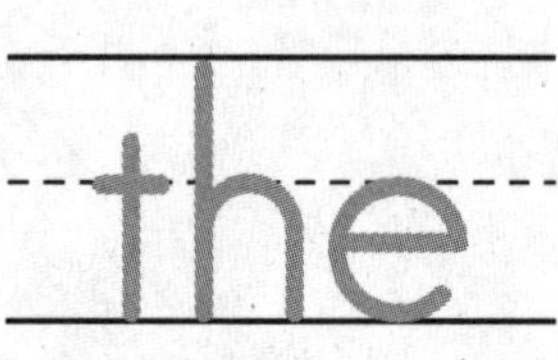

I ▶ **Write I. Draw a picture of something you can do. Read.**

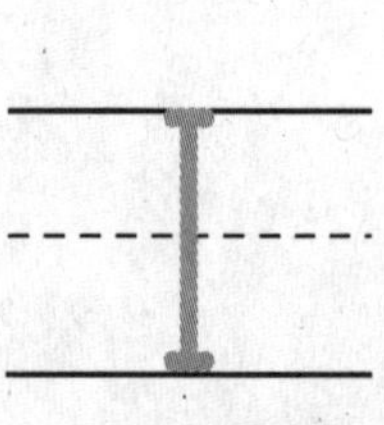

SCHOOL-HOME CONNECTION Ask your child to say each picture name and point to the pictures that begin with the /s/ sound. Have your child practice writing the letters *S* and *s*. Then help your child make up phrases similar to the ones with *the* and *I*.

Name ______________________________

Rr

▶ **Say the name of each picture. If it begins with /r/, write Rr on the lines.**

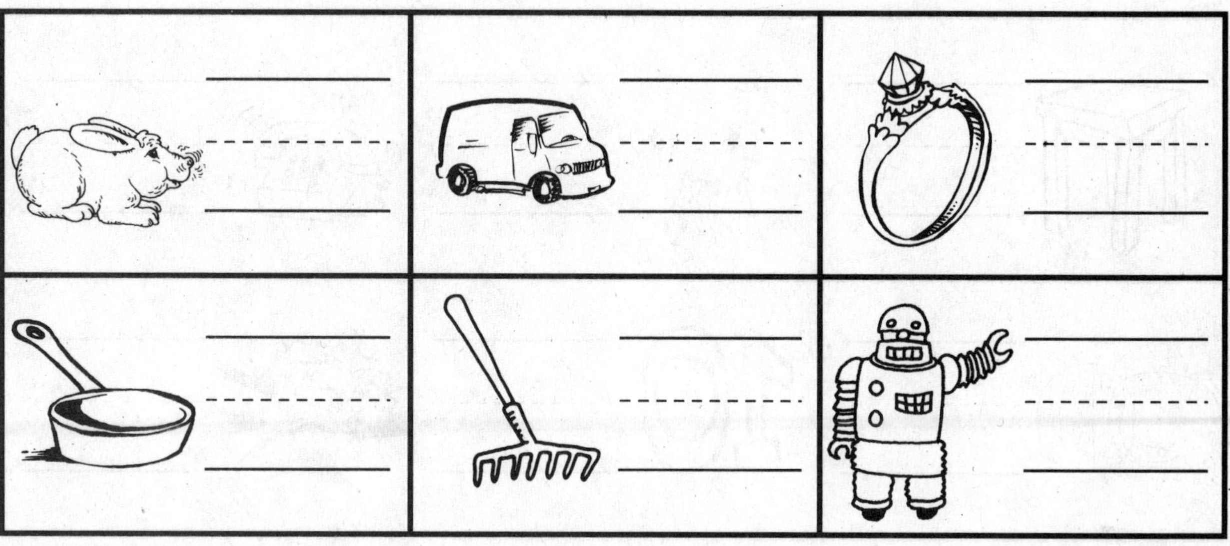

like

▶ **Write like. Draw a picture to finish. Read the sentence.**

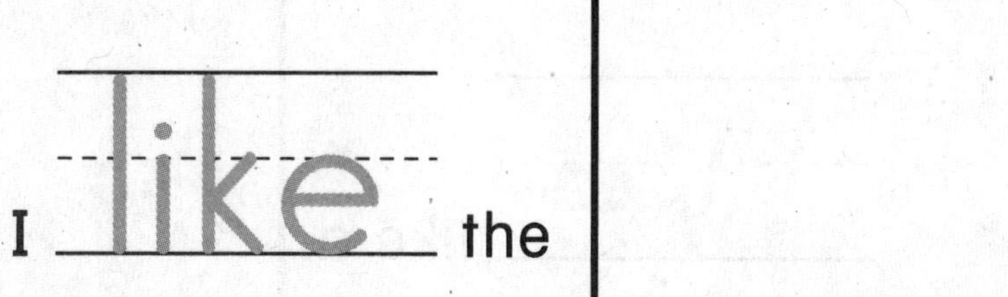

go

▶ **Write go. Draw a picture to finish. Read the sentence.**

SCHOOL-HOME CONNECTION Ask your child to say each picture name and point to the pictures that begin with the /r/ sound. Then help your child make a list of words that begin with *r*. Have your child use some of the words in sentences about things he or she likes.

Name ____________________

Tt

▶ **Say the name of each picture. If it begins with /t/, write Tt on the lines.**

we

▶ **Write we. Draw a picture to finish. Read the sentence.**

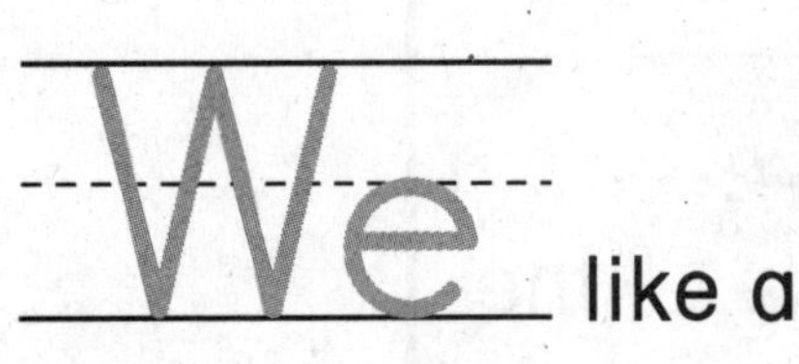 like a ______.

on

▶ **Write on. Draw a picture to finish. Read the sentence.**

I go 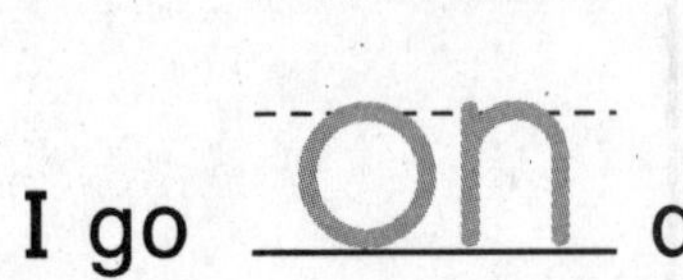 a ______.

SCHOOL-HOME CONNECTION Ask your child to say each picture name and point to the pictures that begin with the /t/ sound. Have your child practice writing the letters *T* and *t*. Then help your child make up sentences similar to the ones with *we* and *on*.

Name ____________________

Pp ▶ **Say the name of each picture. If it begins with /p/, write Pp on the lines.**

Cc ▶ **Say the name of each picture. If it begins with /k/, write Cc on the lines.**

to ▶ **Write to. Draw a picture to finish. Read the sentence.**

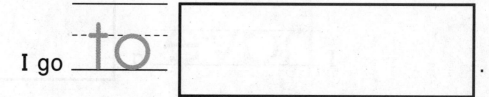

you ▶ **Write you. Draw a picture to finish. Read the sentence.**

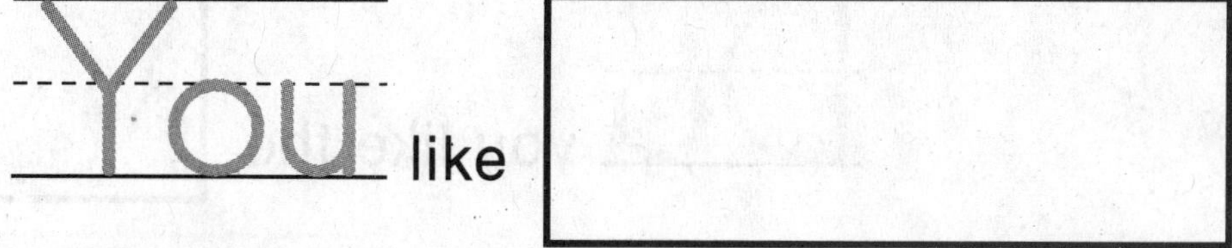

SCHOOL-HOME CONNECTION Ask your child to point to the pictures that begin with the /p/ sound and then the pictures that have the /k/ sound spelled with *c*. Have your child practice writing the letters *P*, *p*, *C*, and *c*. Then together, write sentences with the words *to* and *you*.

Name ______________________________

Inventory Unit

Consonants: /n/n, /d/d
High-Frequency Words: *have, do*

Nn

▶ Say the name of each picture. If it begins with /n/, write Nn on the lines.

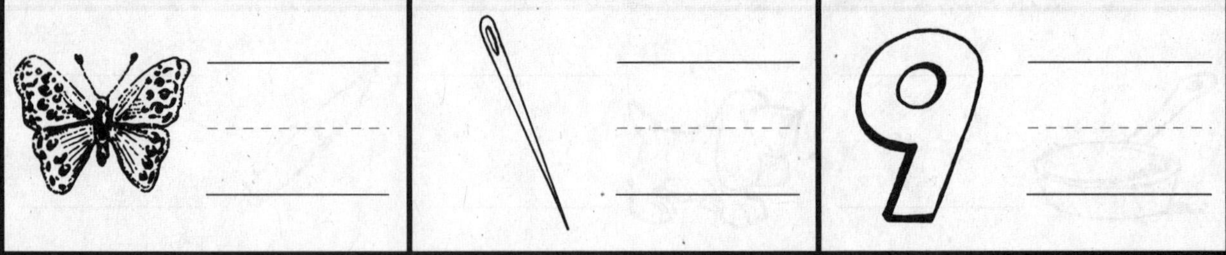

Dd

▶ Say the name of each picture. If it begins with /d/, write Dd on the lines.

have

▶ Write have. Draw a picture to finish. Read the sentence.

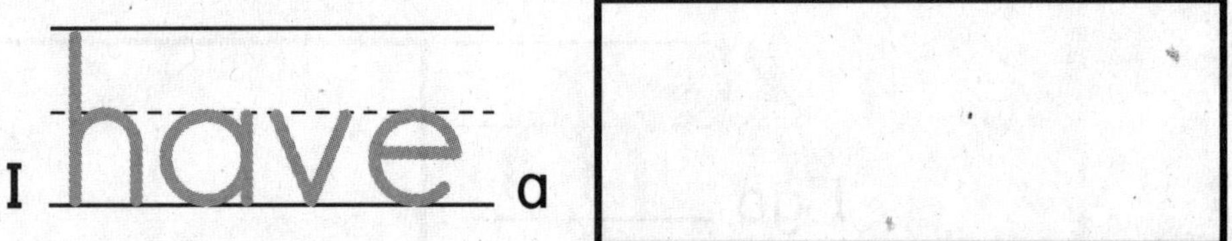

do

▶ Write do. Draw a picture to finish. Read the sentence.

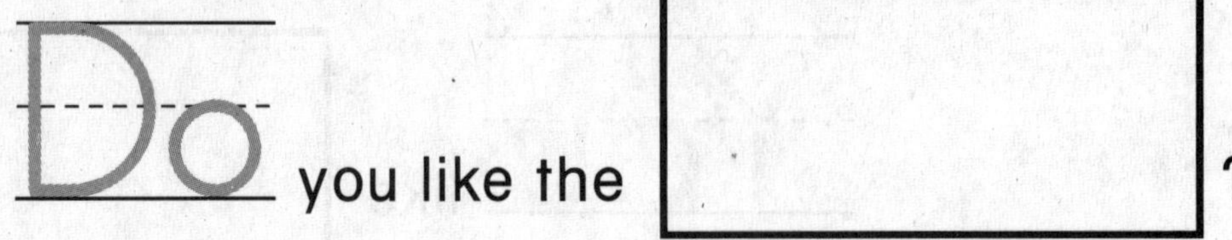

SCHOOL-HOME CONNECTION Ask your child to say each picture name and point to the pictures that begin with the /n/ sound or the /d/ sound. Have your child practice writing the letters *N*, *n*, *D*, and *d*. Then have your child read the sentences to you.

Name ____________________

Gg ▶ **Say the name of each picture. If it begins with /g/, write Gg on the lines.**

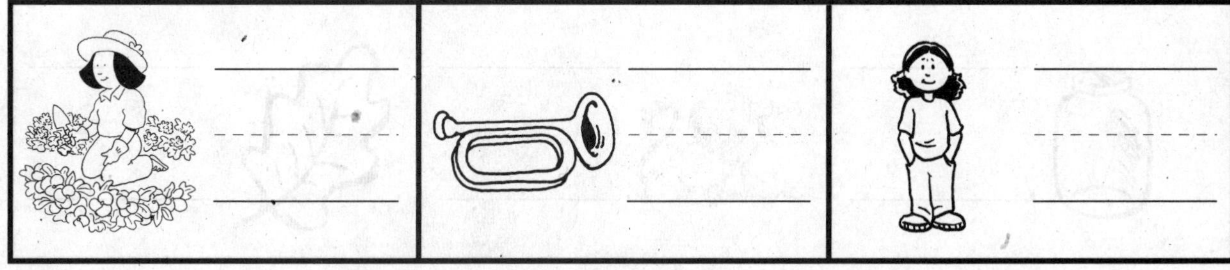

Ff ▶ **Say the name of each picture. If it begins with /f/, write Ff on the lines.**

what ▶ **Write what. Read the question. Then draw a picture to answer it.**

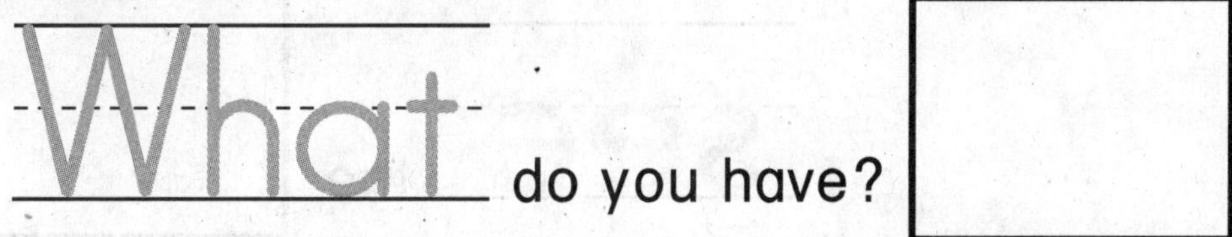

What do you have?

no ▶ **Read the question. Write no. Draw a picture to finish. Then read the sentence.**

Do you like naps?

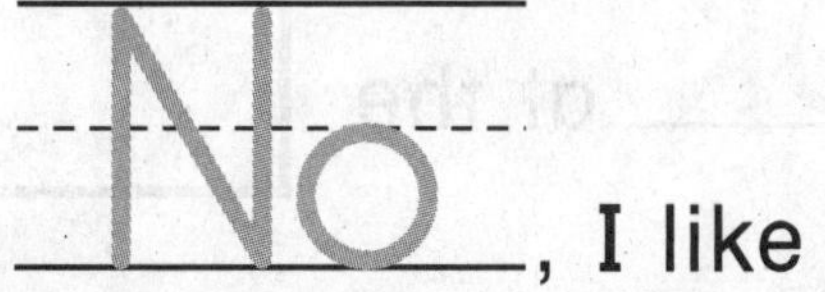

No, I like to ____________.

SCHOOL-HOME CONNECTION Ask your child to say each picture name and point to the pictures that begin with the /g/ sound or the /f/ sound. Then have your child read the sentences to you.

Name ______________________________

Ll

▶ **Say the name of each picture. If it begins with /l/, write Ll on the lines.**

Hh

▶ **Say the name of each picture. If it begins with /h/, write Hh on the lines.**

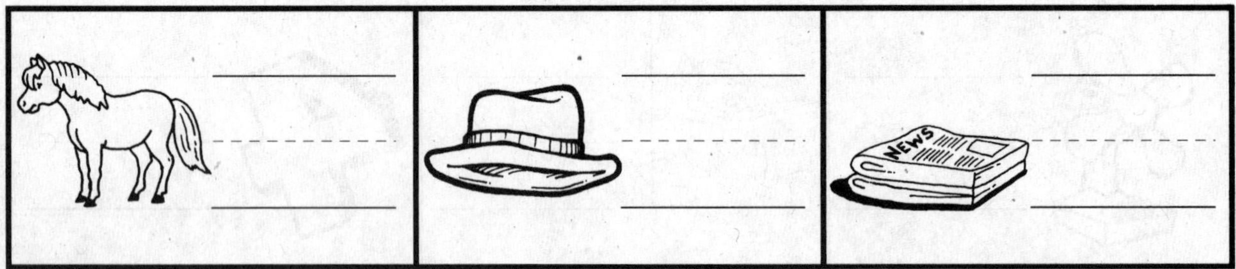

see

▶ **Write see. Draw a picture to finish. Read the sentence.**

I see ______ the ______.

look

▶ **Write Look. Draw a picture to finish. Read the sentence.**

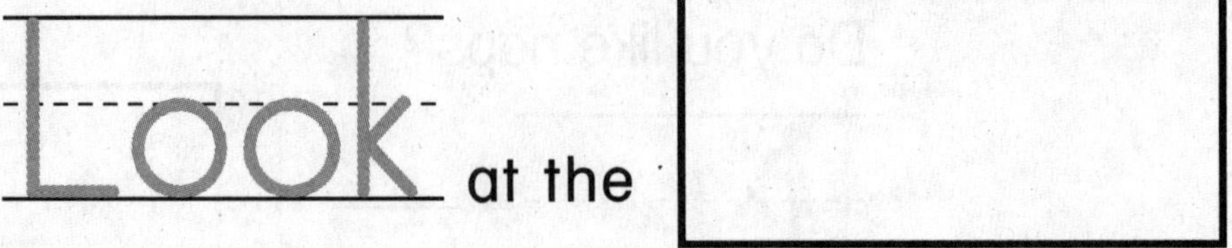

SCHOOL-HOME CONNECTION Ask your child to say each picture name and point to the ones that begin with the /l/ sound or the /h/ sound. Find objects in the house whose names begin with /l/ or /h/.

Name ______________________

Bb

▶ Say the name of each picture. If it begins with /b/, write Bb on the lines.

Kk

▶ Say the name of each picture. If it begins with /k/, write Kk on the lines.

come

▶ Write come. Draw a picture to finish. Read the sentence.

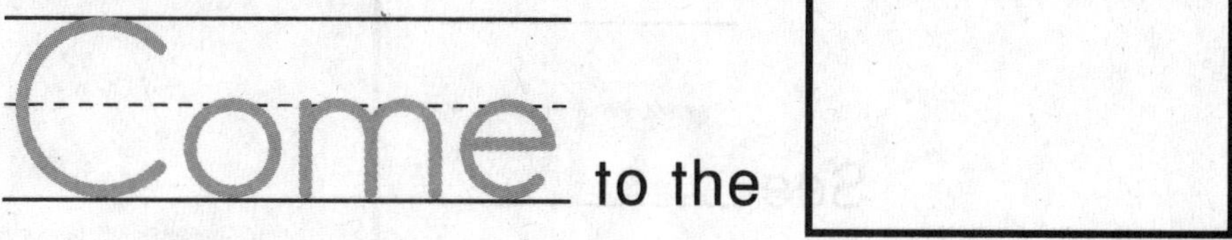

Come to the ______.

for

▶ Write for. Draw a picture to finish. Read the sentence.

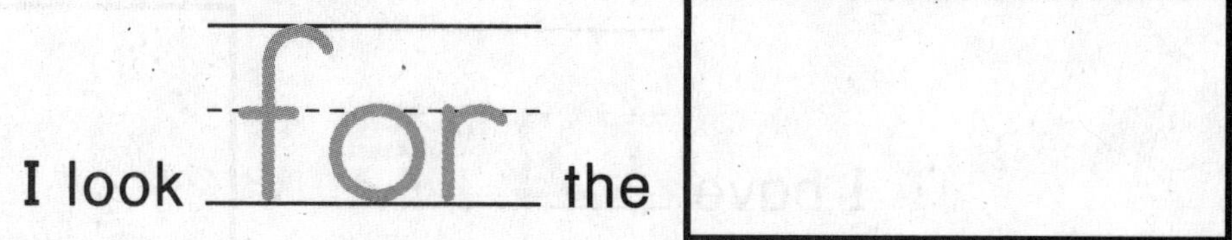

I look for the ______.

SCHOOL-HOME CONNECTION Have your child find objects in your house whose names begin with the /b/ sound or the /k/ sound. Then have your child read the sentences on the page to you. Together, think of more sentences with *Come* and *for*.

Name ______________________

Ww ▶ **Say the name of each picture. If it begins with /w/, write Ww on the lines.**

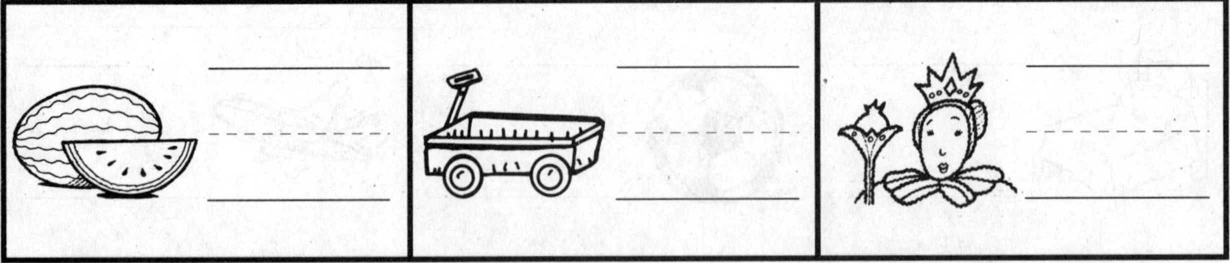

Xx ▶ **Say the name of each picture. If it ends with /ks/, write Xx on the lines.**

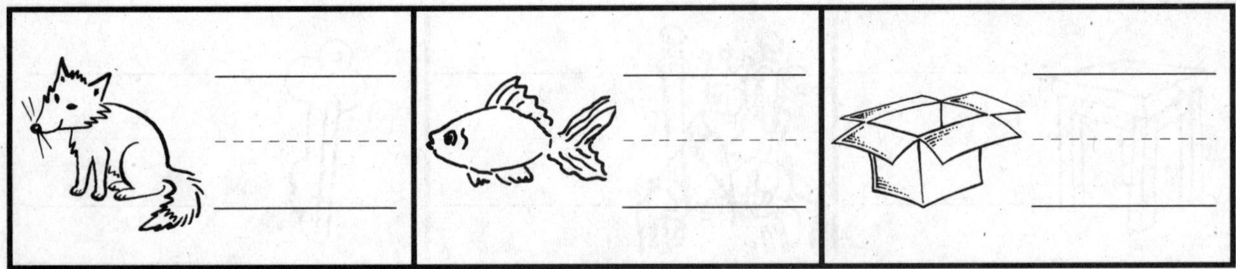

me ▶ **Write me. Draw a picture of something you can do. Read the sentence.**

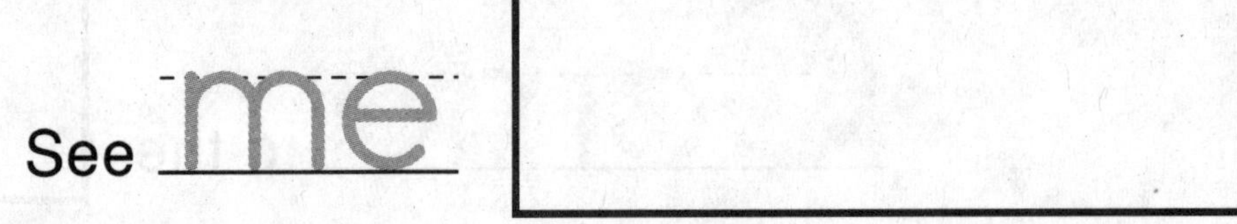

See me ______ .

one ▶ **Write one. Draw a picture to finish. Read the sentence.**

I have one ______ .

SCHOOL-HOME CONNECTION Ask your child to say each picture name and point to the pictures that begin with the /w/ sound or end with the /ks/ sound. Then together, think of more sentences with *me* and *one*.

Name ______________________________

Vv ▶ **Say the name of each picture. If it begins with /v/, write Vv on the lines.**

Jj ▶ **Say the name of each picture. If it begins with /j/, write Jj on the lines.**

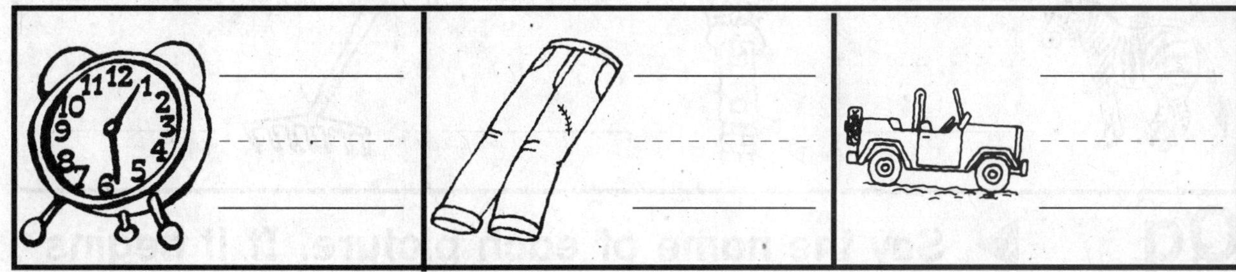

little ▶ **Write little. Draw a picture to finish. Read the sentences.**

I have a little ______.

I have a ______ ______.

SCHOOL-HOME CONNECTION Ask your child to say each picture name and point to the pictures that begin with the /v/ sound or the /j/ sound. Then have your child read the sentences to you. Together, think of more sentences with *little*.

Name ______________________

Inventory Unit

Consonants: /y/y, /z/z; /kw/q
High-Frequency Words: *are, here*

Yy

▶ Say the name of each picture. If it begins with /y/, write Yy on the lines.

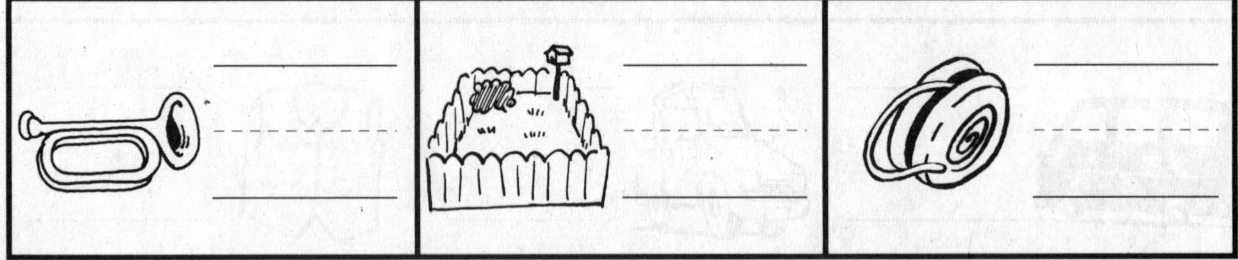

Zz

▶ Say the name of each picture. If it begins with /z/, write Zz on the lines.

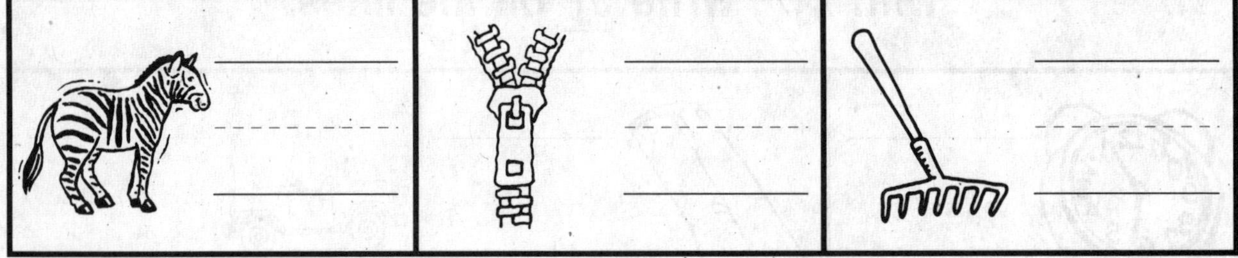

Qq

▶ Say the name of each picture. If it begins with /kw/, write Qq on the lines.

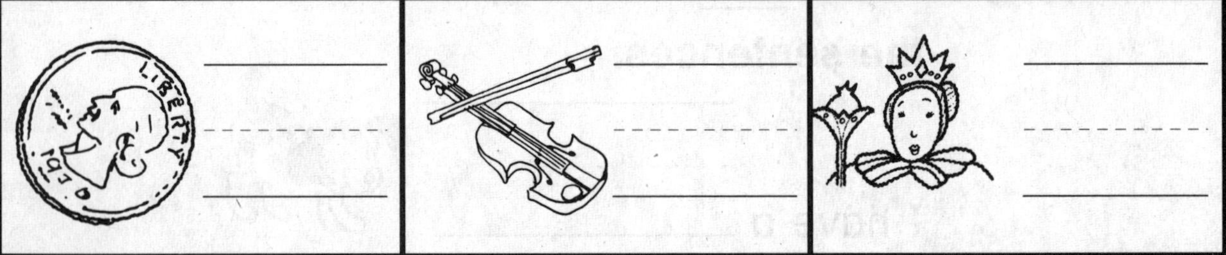

are here

▶ Write are. Write here. Say a sentence for are and here.

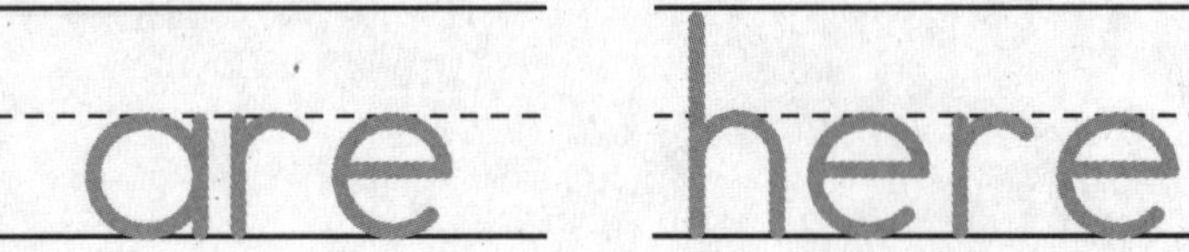

SCHOOL-HOME CONNECTION Ask your child to say each picture name and point to the pictures that begin with the /y/ sound, the /z/ sound, or the /kw/ sounds. Then have your child say a sentence with *are* and *here*. Together, think of more sentences with *are* and *here*.

· TROPHIES ·

Level One

Guess Who

Name ____________________

▶ **Read the words. Then read the name of each group. Write each word in the group where it belongs.**

Words With a

Word Without a

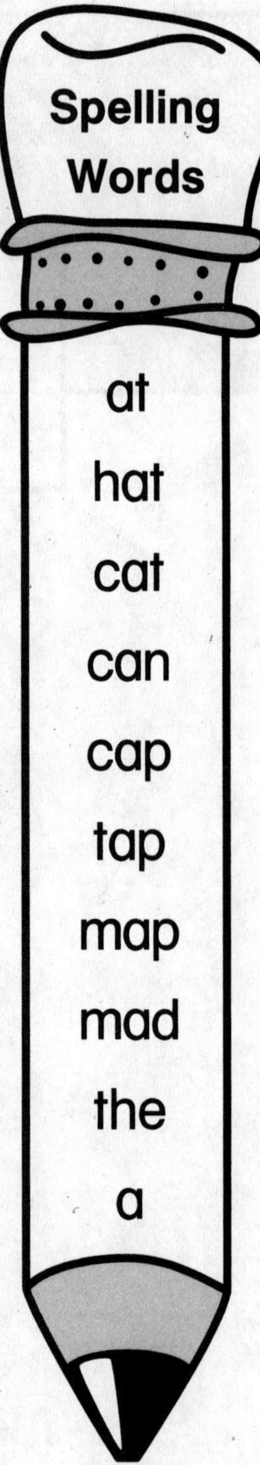

Spelling Words
at
hat
cat
can
cap
tap
map
mad
the
a

SCHOOL-HOME CONNECTION Point to and read each Spelling Word aloud with your child. Talk about what is the same and different about the words.

Name ________________________________

▶ **Say the name of each picture. Circle the picture if the name has the /a/ sound.**

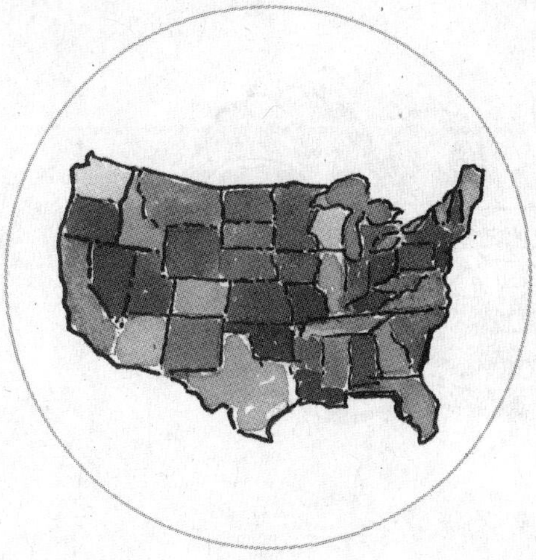

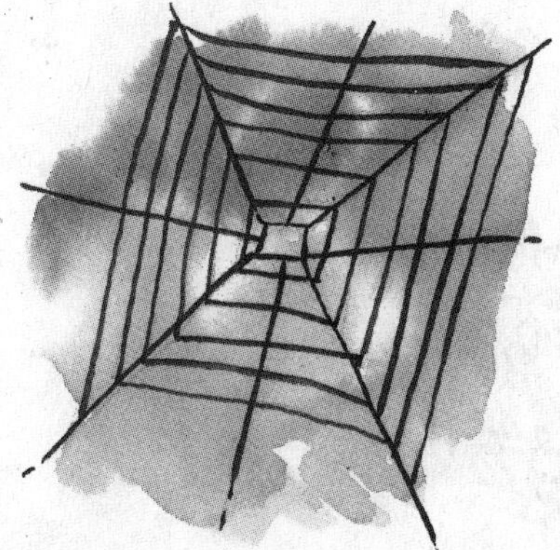

SCHOOL-HOME CONNECTION Ask your child to name the pictures whose names have short vowel *a*. Find at least one more object in the house whose name has the short *a* sound.

Name ______________________________

▶ **Say a sentence to tell what happens in each picture.**

1.

2.

3.

4.

SCHOOL-HOME CONNECTION With your child, take turns saying a few short sentences. Discuss the concept that a sentence tells a complete thought.

Name ______________________________

▶ **Say the name of each picture. Circle the picture if the name has the /a/ sound.**

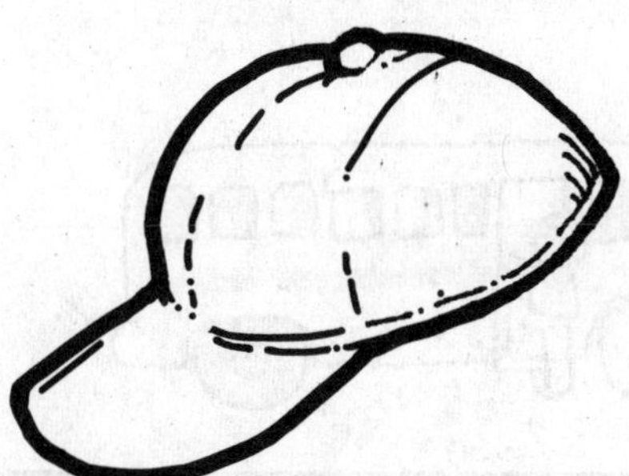

SCHOOL-HOME CONNECTION Ask your child to name the pictures with short vowel *a* and find two words that rhyme. Then have your child say another word that rhymes with those words.

Name ______________________________

Write a word from the box to finish each sentence.

down	got	up

1. Dan ____________ on.

2. Dan sat ____________.

3. A man ____________ on.

4. Dan got ____________.

5. The man sat ____________.

SCHOOL-HOME CONNECTION Write the words *up* and *down* on slips of paper. Make a total of eight cards. Mix up the cards and place them face down on a table. While seated, turn over the top card. If it reads *up*, stand up. If it reads *down*, sit on the floor.

Name ______________________

▶ **Look at each picture. Write the word that completes the sentence.**

am ham

1. I ________ Max.

has as

2. Max ________ a cap.

can am

3. I ________ Jan.

am hat

4. Jan has a ________.

cat bat

5. The ________ has the hat.

SCHOOL-HOME CONNECTION With your child, write about what Max and Jan did next. Read the story. Then make a list of words with short *a*. Read the list together.

Name ______________________

Write 1, 2, and 3 to put the pictures in order.

1.

2.

SCHOOL-HOME CONNECTION Have your child tell you what is happening in each set of pictures. Ask: *What happened first? What happened next? What happened last? How do you know?*

Name ________________________________

▶ **Say each picture name. If the name rhymes with <u>tap</u>, write <u>ap</u>. If the name rhymes with <u>sat</u>, write <u>at</u>.**

1.

2.

3.

4.

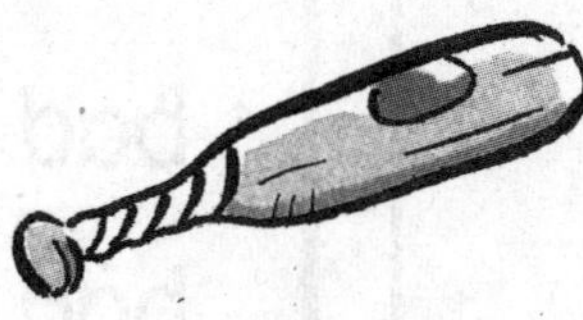

5

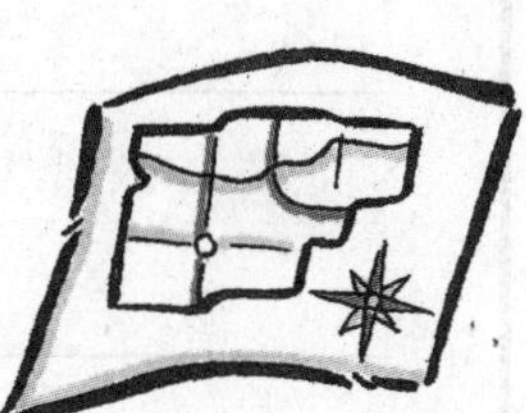

6.

7.

8.

9.

SCHOOL-HOME CONNECTION With your child, make up a short rhyme using words that end with *at* and *ap*.

Name ______________________

▶ **Read the words. Then read the name of each group. Write each word in the group where it belongs.**

Words With a

______________________ | ______________________

______________________ | ______________________

______________________ | ______________________

______________________ | ______________________

______________________ | ______________________

______________________ | ______________________

______________________ | ______________________

______________________ | ______________________

Words Without a

______________________ | ______________________

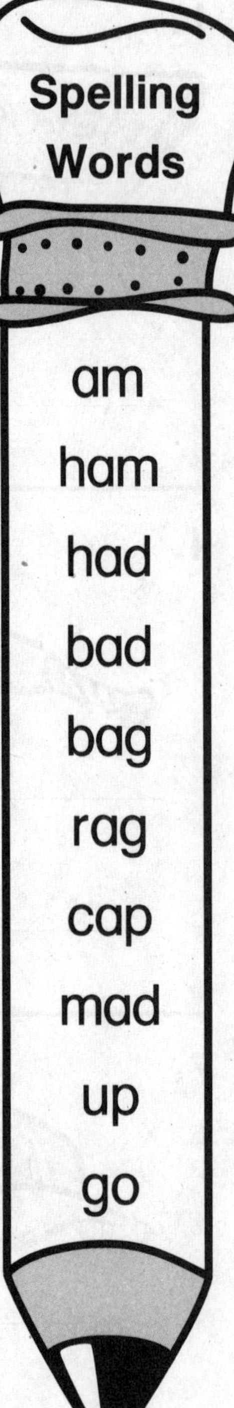

Spelling Words
am
ham
had
bad
bag
rag
cap
mad
up
go

SCHOOL-HOME CONNECTION Point to and read each Spelling Word aloud with your child. Talk about what is the same and different about the words. Ask your child to name and write other words that have only two letters.

Name ____________________

The picture names in each row rhyme. Write the rhyming words.

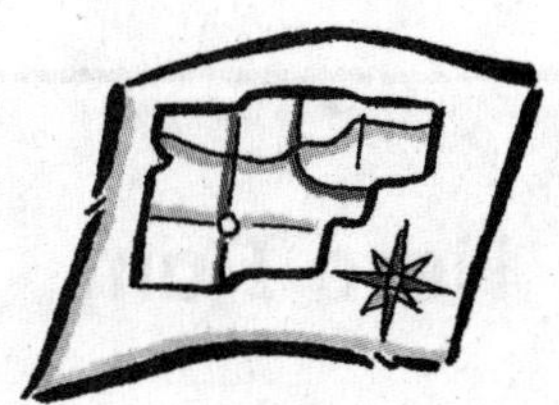

1. cap ____________ ____________

2. can ____________ ____________

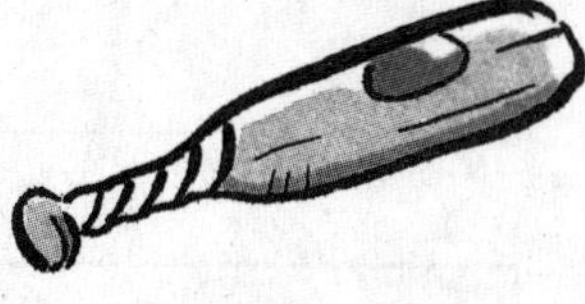

3. hat ____________ ____________

SCHOOL-HOME CONNECTION Ask your child to find and name things in your home that rhyme with *cap*, *can*, and *hat*.

Name ______________________________

▶ **Circle each word group that is a sentence. Then write each sentence. Draw a picture to go with the sentences.**

can go **Here I am.** **Sam and Max**

Can Sam come? **up and down** **Sam can go.**

1. ______________________________

2. ______________________________

3. ______________________________

SCHOOL-HOME CONNECTION Let your child point out sentences on this page or in a book. Ask where one sentence ends and the next sentence begins.

Name ______________________________

▶ **Say each picture name. Write the word in the boxes. Each new word will have two letters from the word before it.**

1.  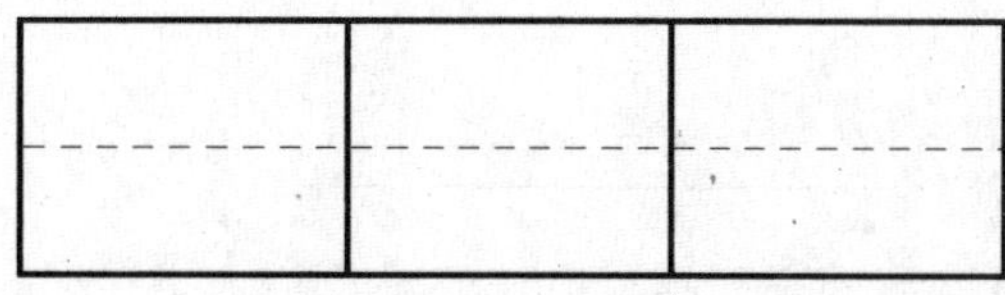

2.  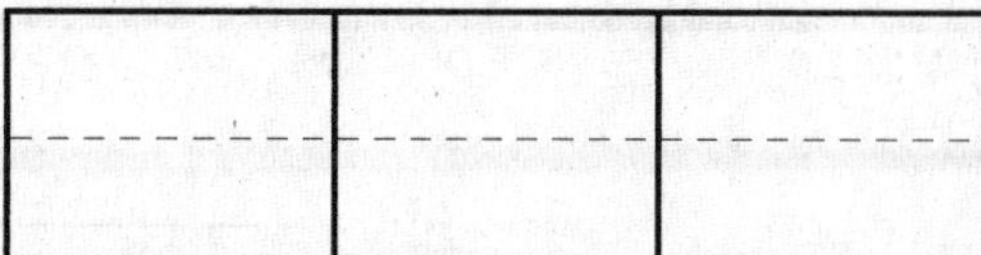

3.  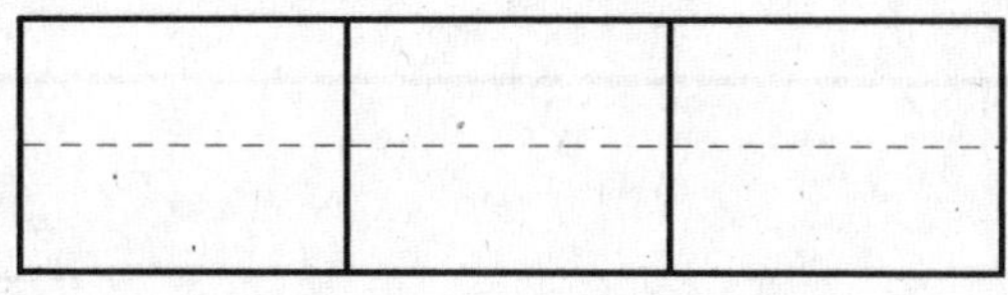

4.  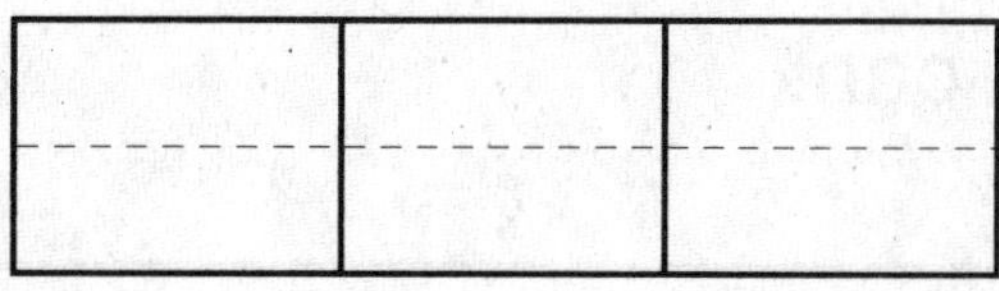

5. 

SCHOOL-HOME CONNECTION Ask your child to name the word that rhymes with *bat*. Then ask him or her what other words rhyme with *bat* and *cat*. List the words. Repeat for *can* and *man*.

Name ______________________

▶ **Write a word from the box to finish each sentence.**

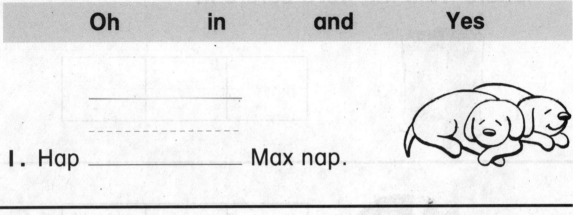

Oh	in	and	Yes

1. Hap __________ Max nap.

2. Hap and Max nap __________ a hat.

3. Can Dan have the hat? __________, he can.

4. __________, no! My hat!

SCHOOL-HOME CONNECTION Write the words on slips of paper to make word cards. Make two sets. Mix up the cards and place them face down. Play "Concentration." Take turns turning over pairs of cards and reading the words. Players keep pairs that match.

Name ______________________________

▶ **Write the words from the box where they belong in the puzzle.**

tag	man	mat	cap	pan

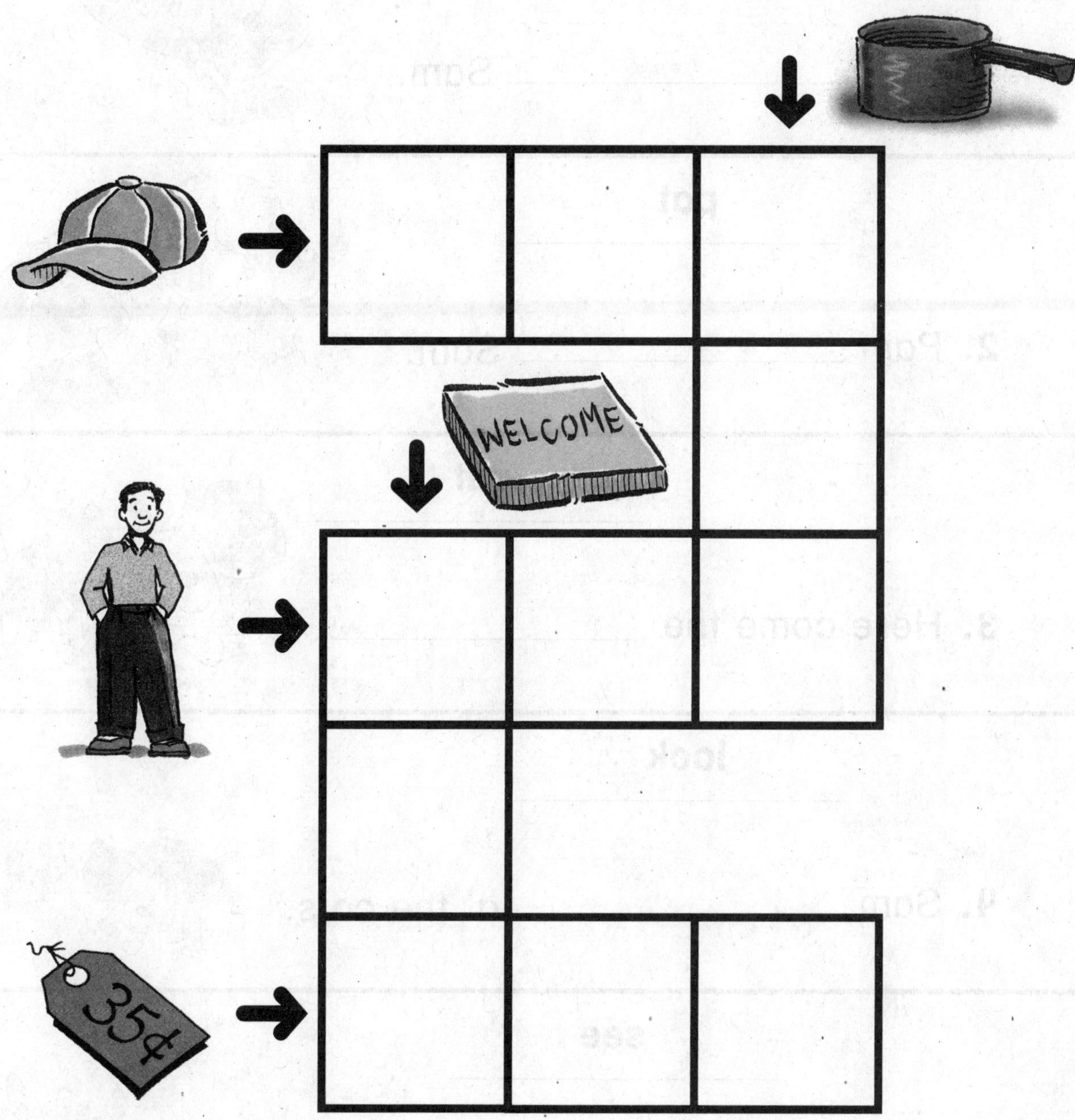

SCHOOL-HOME CONNECTION Ask what sound your child hears in the middle of each word. Together, think of other words with the same sound.

Name ______________________________

▶ **Finish each sentence. Add s to the word above the line. Write the new word.**

come

1. Here ______________ Sam.

pat

2. Pam ______________ Sam.

cat

3. Here come the ______________.

look

4. Sam ______________ at the cats.

see

5. One cat ______________ Sam.

SCHOOL-HOME CONNECTION Write the words *hat* and *hats*. Ask your child to tell you how the two words are different. With your child, make up a sentence using both words.

Name ______________________

▶ **Read the words. Then read the name of each group. Write each word in the group where it belongs.**

Words With i	Words With a

Words Without i or a

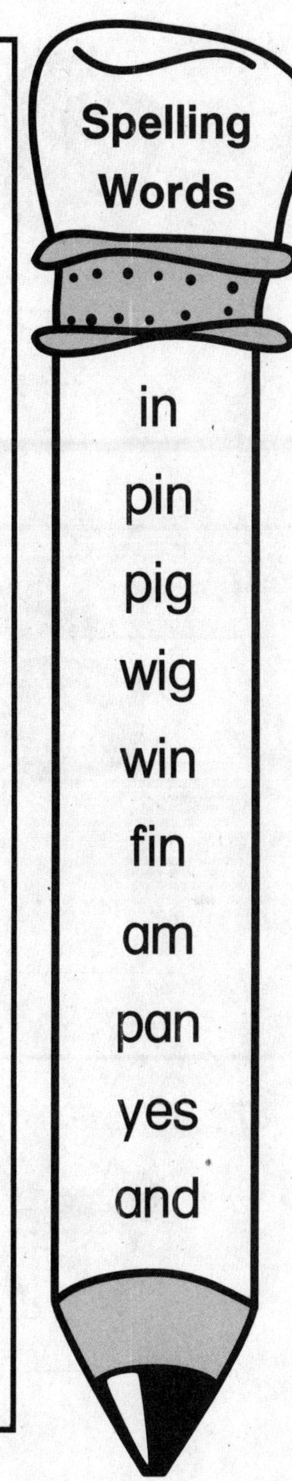

Spelling Words
in
pin
pig
wig
win
fin
am
pan
yes
and

SCHOOL-HOME CONNECTION Point to each Spelling Word and have your child read it to you. Talk about the words. Ask how *in* and *am* are different than the other words.

Name ___________________________

▶ **Name each picture. Listen for the sound in the middle of the word. Write i if you hear the sound /i/.**

1. 

2. 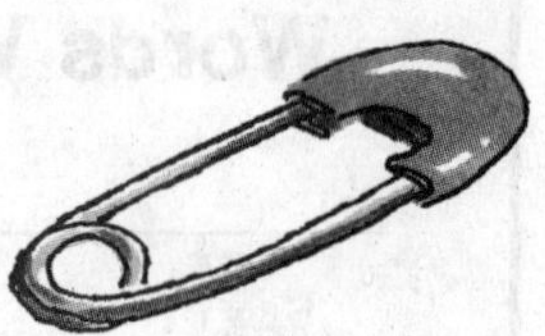

3. 

4. 

5. 

6. 

7. 

8. 

9. 

SCHOOL-HOME CONNECTION Ask your child to identify the letter that stands for the sound that begins the word *igloo*. Have your child practice writing that letter.

Name ______________________________

▶ **Sam's words are all mixed up. Write the words in order.**

1. Sam am I.

2. sat I here.

3. here. sat Tim

4. cat here. A sat

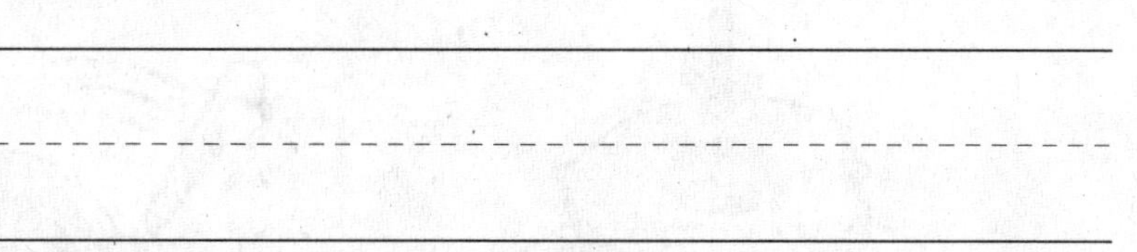

Draw a picture of yourself. Make up a sentence about it. Say your words in order.

SCHOOL-HOME CONNECTION Say a short sentence. Mix up the order of two words in your sentence. Ask your child to say the sentence with the words in the right order.

Name ______________________________

▶ **The picture names in each row rhyme.**
Write the rhyming words.

1. p<u>ig</u> ______________ ______________

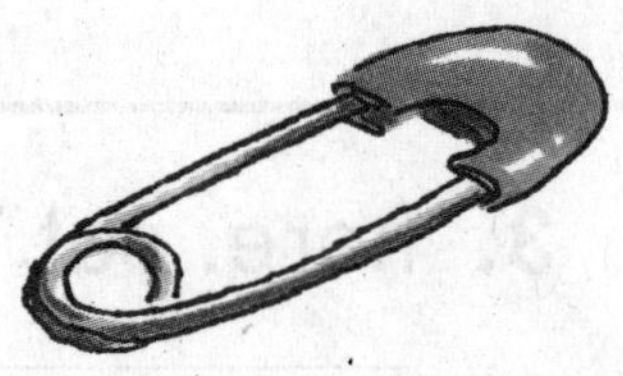

2. f<u>in</u> ______________ ______________

3. s<u>it</u> ______________ ______________

SCHOOL-HOME CONNECTION Read the words with your child. Take turns naming other words that rhyme with *fin*. Make a list of your words.

Name ______________________________

▶ **Write a word from the box to finish each sentence.**

walk	they	make

1. Sal and Liz ____________ a gift for Dan.

2. Sal and Liz ____________ to see Dan.

3. What did ____________ make?

4. Did you ____________ it for me?

SCHOOL-HOME CONNECTION Write the words *make*, *they*, and *walk* on pieces of paper. Put the words face down and mix them up. Let your child pick a word, read it, and say a sentence using the word.

Name ______________________________

▶ **Write the word from the box that names each picture.**

hit	hill	pin	kiss	bib	milk

1. ______________

2. ______________

3. ______________

4. ______________

5. ______________

6. ______________

SCHOOL-HOME CONNECTION Ask your child to read the words he or she wrote. Ask what sound these words all share. Then ask your child to use one or more of the words in a sentence.

Name ____________________

▶ **Look at the picture. Then write a word from the box to complete each sentence.**

cat	bat	pig

1. The __________ is big.

2. The __________ is little.

3. The __________ has a hat.

SCHOOL-HOME CONNECTION Have your child read aloud the sentences she or he completed. Then ask your child to tell you about other details in the picture.

Name ________________

▶ **Read the contractions in the box. Finish each sentence. Write the contraction for the two words above the lines.**

Here's	Pat's	It's	What's

Pat is

1. ____________ here.

Here is

2. ____________ a sack.

It is

3. ____________ for Pat.

What is

4. ____________ in it?

SCHOOL-HOME CONNECTION Ask your child to point to two words he or she wrote as a contraction. Together, think of other pairs of words that can be written as contractions.

Name ______________________

▶ **Read the words. Then read the name of each group. Write each word in the group where it belongs.**

Words With i	Words With a
______	______
______	______
______	______
______	______
______	______
______	______

Word Without a or i

______

Spelling Words

pick
pack
tack
back
sack
sick
big
is
they
walk

SCHOOL-HOME CONNECTION Point to and read each Spelling Word aloud with your child. Talk about how the words are alike and different. Ask your child which words rhyme.

Name ____________________

▶ **Write the word from the box that names each picture.**

Jack	sack	sick	tack	kick	pack

1. ____________________

2. ____________________

3. ____________________

4. ____________________

5. ____________________

6. ____________________ and Jill

TRY THIS Write a word that begins or ends with the /k/ sound. Draw a picture to go with the word.

SCHOOL-HOME CONNECTION Have your child point out words that begin or end with the /k/ sound. Together, think of other words that begin or end with that sound.

Name ______

▶ **Write these telling sentences correctly.**

1. look at the hat

2. i see a cat

3. the cat is on the hat

4. the cat will sit and sit

TRY THIS! Write a telling sentence about your favorite food.

SCHOOL-HOME CONNECTION Ask your child to say a few sentences about a cat. Write the sentences. Have your child point out the capital letters and periods.

Name ________________________

Look at the pictures. Write the word from the box that completes each sentence.

kick	Nick	pack	pick

1\. Jack can ____________.

2\. ____________ can nap.

3\. Pam can ____________.

4\. Dan can ____________.

SCHOOL-HOME CONNECTION Ask your child to point out the word *kick* on this page. Encourage your child to say other words that end with the same sound.

Name ____________________

▶ Write a word from the box to complete each sentence.

help	now	play	too	want

1. Will you ____________?

No, I want to ____________.

2. Will you ____________?

No, I want to play, ____________.

3. Can we help ____________?

4. We ____________ to help you.

SCHOOL-HOME CONNECTION Ask your child to say a sentence using one of the words in the box. Write the sentence. Your child can draw a picture for the sentence.

Name ______________________________

▶ **Write the words where they belong in the puzzles.**

kick **pick** **sack** **pack** **sick**

1.

2.

3.

4.

5.

1. ↓

2. →

4. ↓

3. →

5. →

SCHOOL-HOME CONNECTION Let your child read aloud the words he or she wrote in the crossword puzzles. Then ask your child to say words that end with the same sound.

Name ________________________________

▶ **Write 1, 2, and 3 to put the pictures in order.**

▶ **Draw a picture to show what might happen next.**

SCHOOL-HOME CONNECTION Let your child tell you the story in the pictures on this page. Ask, *"Why wouldn't the story make sense if you mixed up the order?"*

Name ______________________________

▶ **Complete each sentence. Write the contraction for the two words above the line.**

I will

1. ______________ play in the band.

I will

2. ______________ play in the band, too.

You will

3. ______________ play in the band, too!

We will

4. ______________ ask Mom and Dad to come.

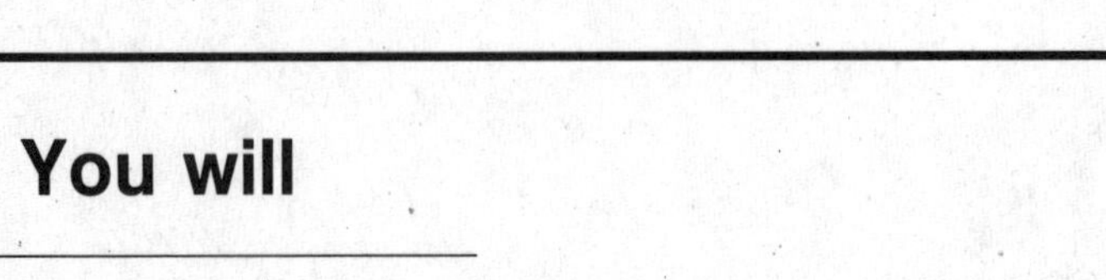

You will

5. ______________ come to see the band play.

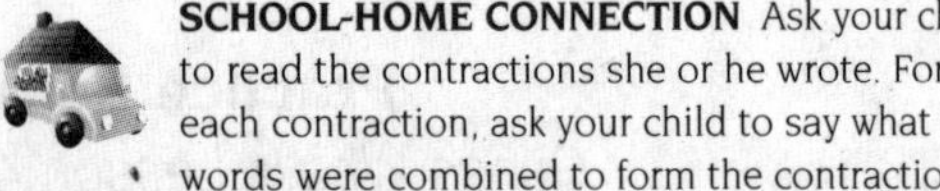

SCHOOL-HOME CONNECTION Ask your child to read the contractions she or he wrote. For each contraction, ask your child to say what two words were combined to form the contraction.

Name ______________________________

▶ **Read the words. Then read the name of each group. Write each word in the group where it belongs.**

Words With o

Words Without o

Spelling Words

hot
hop
pop
pot
dot
not
back
pick
now
want

SCHOOL-HOME CONNECTION Point to each Spelling Word, and have your child read it. Talk about how the words are alike and how they are different. Ask your child which of the words rhyme.

Name ____________________

▶ **Say each picture name. Color the picture if the name has the sound /o/.**

1.	2.	3.

4.	5.	6.
		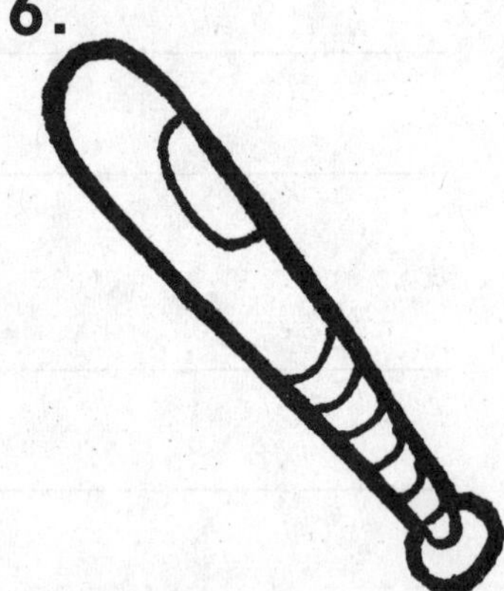
7.	8.	9.
	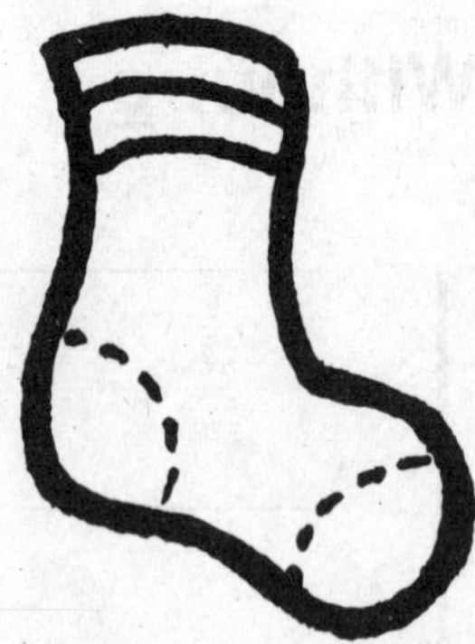	

SCHOOL-HOME CONNECTION Find things in the house whose names have the short *o* sound as in *on*. Let your child hop from one short *o* object to the next.

Name ______________________

Write these asking sentences correctly.

1. what do you want

2. did you see that

3. can Dad do that

4. what will you do

Read the sentences. Circle the asking sentence. Underline the telling sentence.

Are they here? **They are here.**

TRY THIS! Write your own asking sentence. Use a capital letter and a question mark.

SCHOOL-HOME CONNECTION Help your child identify asking sentences: Write questions. Have your child write the question mark for each one.

Name ______________________

▶ **Look at each picture. Circle the word that completes the sentence. Then write the word.**

sacks socks

1. The ______________ are on the mat.

cot got

2. The dolls are on the ______________.

pop top

3. The caps are on ______________.

pats pots

4. The lids are on the ______________.

SCHOOL-HOME CONNECTION Ask your child to read the words he or she wrote. Look for things in the house whose names have the short *o* vowel sound, as in *on*.

Name ______________________

High-Frequency Words

Todd's Box

▶ **Write a word from the box to complete each sentence.**

Don't	of	so

1. We are ____________ fast!

2. ____________ sit here, Rick!

3. We will hop a lot ____________ hops.

4. I am ____________ hot!
Me too!

Draw a picture that shows what might happen next. Write a sentence about your picture.

SCHOOL-HOME CONNECTION Read the sentences with your child. Discuss your child's ideas about what might happen next. Encourage your child to draw and write about her or his ideas.

Name ______________________________

Look at each picture. Write the word that completes the sentence.

sit sock

1. Tim and Tom __________ in the pond.

jack jog

2. Ron and Dot __________ to the pond.

pop pond

3. Will Ron and Dot go in the __________?

log lock **rob rock**

4. Tim is on a __________. Tom is on a __________.

lick kick

5. Dot and Ron __________ in the pond.

SCHOOL-HOME CONNECTION With your child, make up a story about what the turtle and rabbit friends did next. Write and read the story with your child.

Name ______________________________

▶ **Put together the word and the word ending. Write the new word to complete the sentence.**

look + ed

1. Dan ____________ for me.

look + ing

2. Now I am ____________ for him.

help + ed

3. Dan ____________ me.

help + ing

4. Now I am ____________ him.

do + ing

5. What is Dan ____________?

SCHOOL-HOME CONNECTION Have your child read aloud one of the sentences he or she completed. Ask how the word above the line changed. Encourage your child to make up other sentences using that word.

Name ______________________________

▶ **Read the words. Then read the name of each group. Write each word in the group where it belongs.**

Words With a	Words With o

Spelling Words

all
call
fall
wall
ball
tall
on
not
so
of

SCHOOL-HOME CONNECTION Point to each Spelling Word and read it with your child. Ask your child to think of other words that rhyme with *all* and *not*. Make a list of each set of rhyming words. Let your child read the words to you.

Name ___________________________

Phonics

Vowel Variant: /ô/a

▶ **Write a word from the box to complete each sentence.**

all	ball	fall	hall	mall

1. Dad and Liz go to the ________.

2. Can I hop down the ________?

3. No. I don't want you to ________.

4. We can kick a ________.

5. We can ________ play ball!

SCHOOL-HOME CONNECTION Have your child write the word *all* on a slip of paper. Write the letters *b, c, f, h, m,* and *t* on a piece of paper. Have your child place the *all* card next to each letter and read the new word.

Name ______________________________

Write the naming part of each sentence.

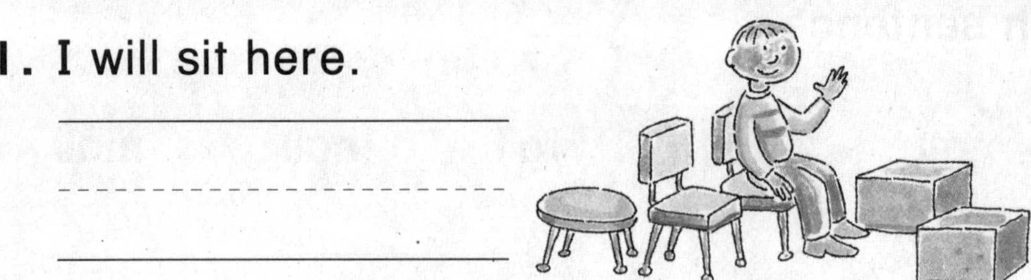

1. I will sit here.

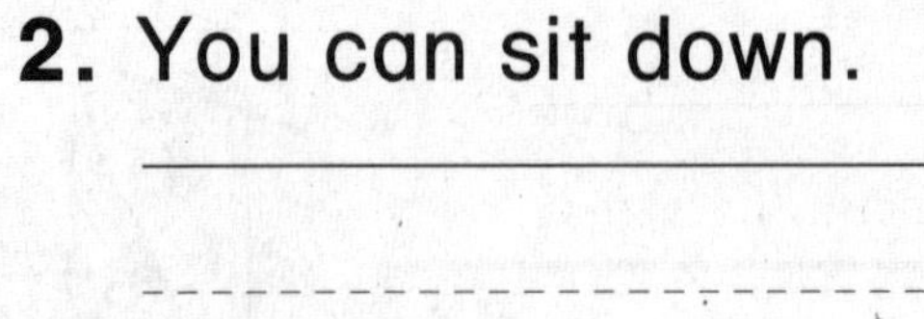

2. You can sit down.

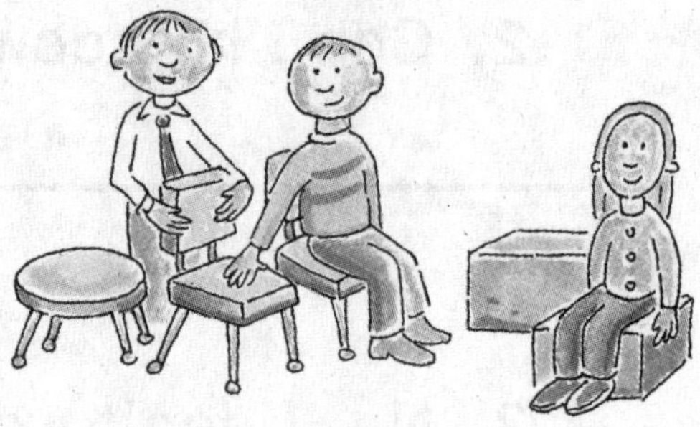

3. My dad can sit here.

4. Matt can sit here.

5. His dog will sit here.

TRY THIS Choose one of the naming parts you wrote. Use it to begin another sentence. Write the new sentence.

SCHOOL-HOME CONNECTION Ask your child to tell you what the naming part of a sentence does. Then have your child say several sentences with the naming part *I*.

Name ______________________

Phonics
Vowel Variant: /ô/a

▶ **Circle the word that completes each sentence. Then write the word.**

1. The dogs are in the ________. **hill** **hall** **call**

2. Can ________ the dogs pass? **call** **all** **ill**

3. One dog is too ________. **lit** **tall** **all**

4. I ________ the big dog Mack. **call** **ill** **mall**

5. Are ________ the dogs in now? **hall** **mall** **all**

SCHOOL-HOME CONNECTION Ask your child to write the word *all*. Together, think of words that rhyme with *all*.

Name ___________________________

▶ **Write a word from the box to complete each sentence.**

Where	that	very	buy

1. __________ are we going?

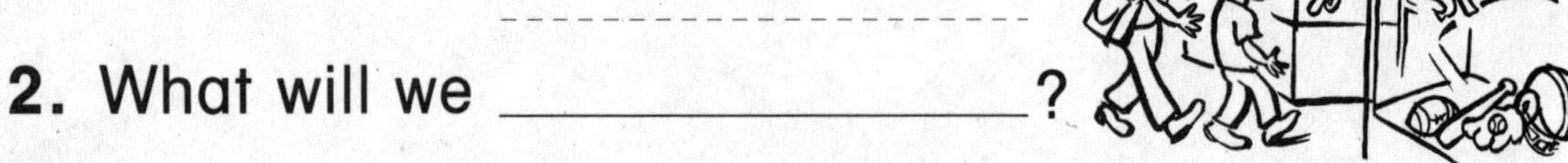

2. What will we __________?

3. Dad wants __________ fishing rod.

4. Kim likes a __________ big bat.

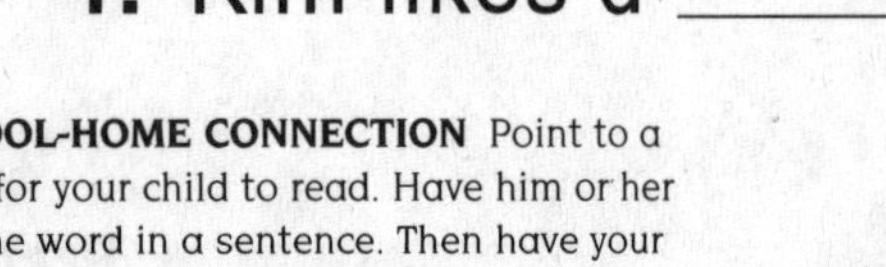

SCHOOL-HOME CONNECTION Point to a word for your child to read. Have him or her use the word in a sentence. Then have your child point to a word. Read it and make up a sentence. Take turns reading words and making up sentences.

Name ______________________________

▶ **Write the words where they belong in the puzzle.**

pill	doll	wall	fall

1.

2.

3.

4.

1. ↓

3. ↓

2. →

4. →

SCHOOL-HOME CONNECTION Draw four boxes in a row. Write *ll* in the last two boxes. Have your child fill in the first two letters and read the word to you.

Name ___

▶ **Write 1, 2, and 3 to put the sentences and pictures in order. Then draw a picture. Show what might happen next.**

Ken looks for a box. ___

Ken looks into the box. ___

Ken sees a big box. ___

SCHOOL-HOME CONNECTION Have your child tell you what is happening in the pictures. Ask about the picture your child drew.

Name ______________________

Finish each sentence. Write the contraction for the two words.

didn't	isn't	don't	hasn't	aren't

is not

1. Tim ______________ here.

did not

2. Dan ______________ call him.

are not

3. Dan's pals ______________ here.

do not

4. I ______________ see it.

has not

5. It ______________ come.

SCHOOL-HOME CONNECTION Ask your child to write the contraction *didn't*. Ask which two words are joined in that contraction.

Jan's Cat

1

Jan's cat ran.

3

Fold

Jan pats the cat.

8

Fold

Here, Cat! Look!

9

2 **Look!**

Come down, Cat! 7

4 **The cat got up.**

Come down, Cat! 5

Fold

Fold

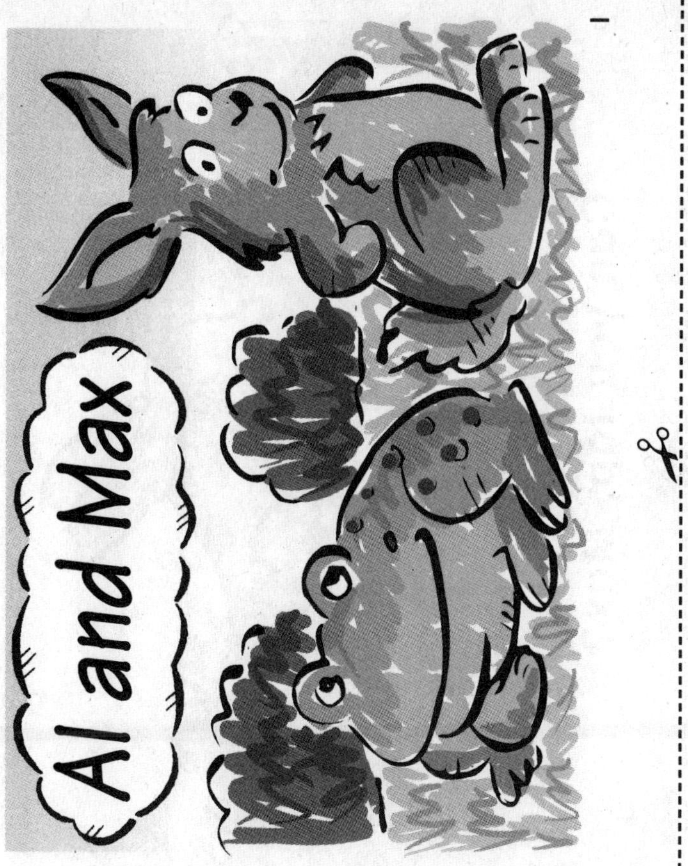

Al and Max

1

Yes. We like to tap.

3

6

No! Max and Al are pals.

8

Fold

Fold

2 **Can you tap, Max?**

Are Al and Max mad? 7

Fold

Al sat. Max sat. 4

Max and Al ran. 5

Tim and Pam

1

Tim can walk.

3

Pam is here.

6

It's Tim! It's Pam!

Pam and Tim make it!

8

Fold

Fold

Pam can walk.

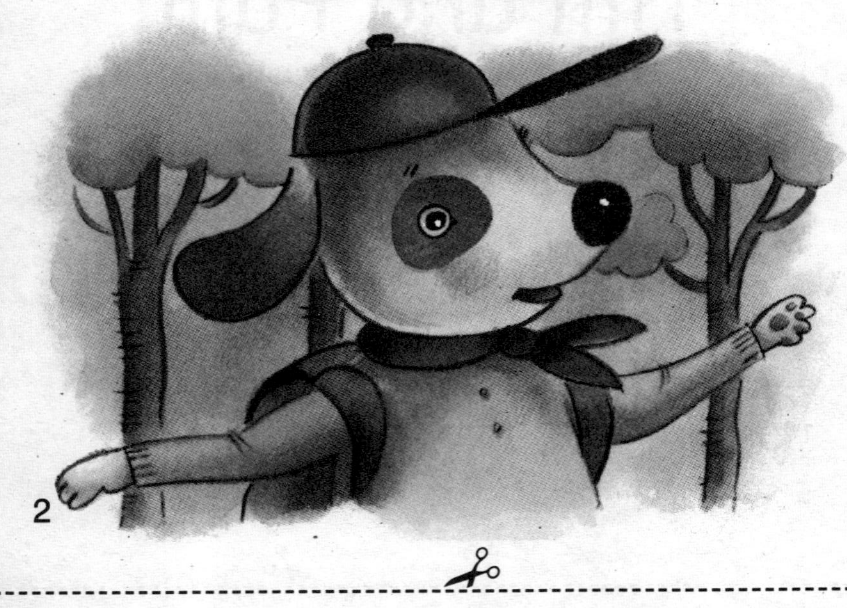

2

Tim has his map.
Pam has a map.

4

Tim is here.

5

They can make it.
They can walk here.

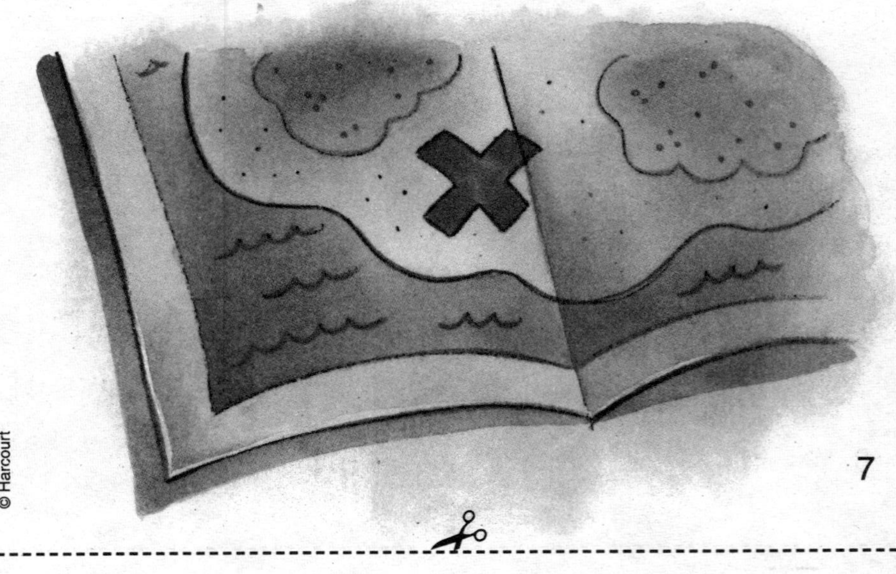

7

Fold

Fold

Mack and Sam

1

See, Mack?

I want to play. 3

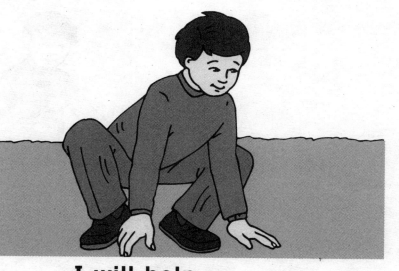

6 I will help.

Sit like me, Mack.

Mack sits.

8 Sam pats him on the back.

Fold

Fold

2 Sam and Mack can play here.

Will Mack sit, too? 7

Fold

Fold

You got it, Mack.
Now come back.

4

Sit, Mack. 5

A Sack for You

1

Tom's sack is big, too.
Is it a sack of rocks?

3

Jill has sacks.
The sacks have
lots of dots.

6

What is in it?

8

Fold

Fold

Kim's sack is so big.
What can fit in it?

2

Here are the sacks.
Pick the sack for you.

7

Fold

Pam has a little sack.
Is it a sack of socks?

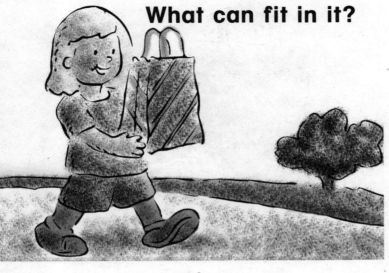

4

The dog has a sack, too.
Dogs don't pack sacks!

5

Fold

One for Me!

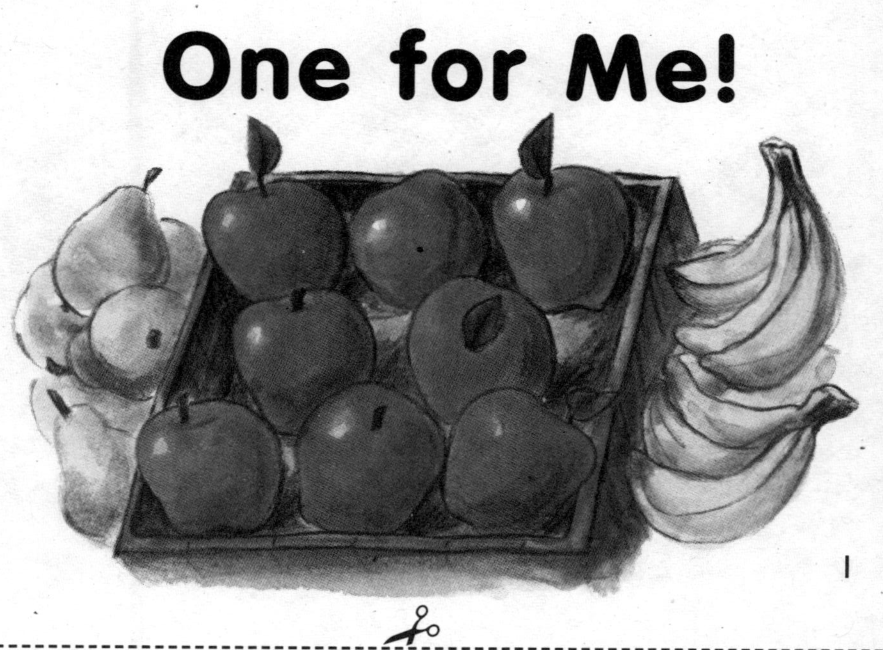

1

Where did they all go? 3

6 I see the box at the store.

8 That's where I got it!

Fold

Fold

2 Look up on that hill.

I want Mom to buy it. 7

Fold

4 A tall man picked and picked.

He packed the box very well. 5

• TROPHIES •

Level Two

Catch a Dream

Name ______________________________

▶ **Read the words. Then read the name of each group. Write each word in the group where it belongs.**

Words With e

Words With a

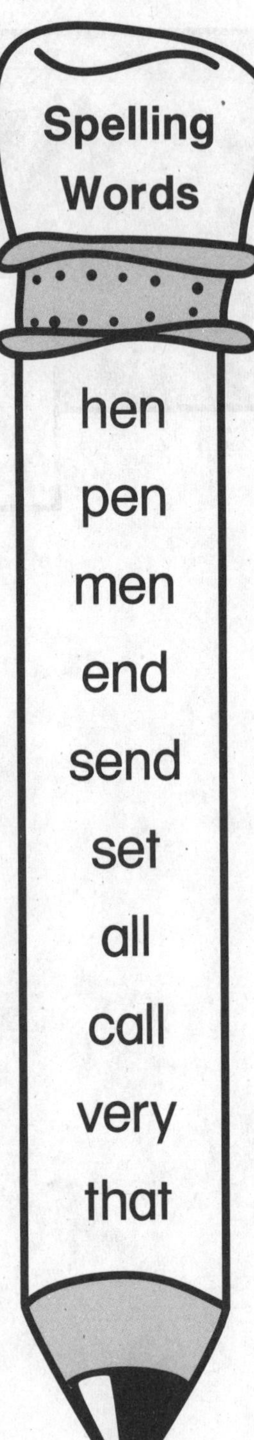

Spelling Words
hen
pen
men
end
send
set
all
call
very
that

SCHOOL-HOME CONNECTION Write the words *pan, and, sand,* and *sit*. Have your child change one letter in each word to make a Spelling Word. (*pen, end, send, set*)

Name ______________________________

▶ **Write the word from the box that names each picture.**

net	bell	pen	desk	tent	bed	men	web	ten

1. 

2. 

3. 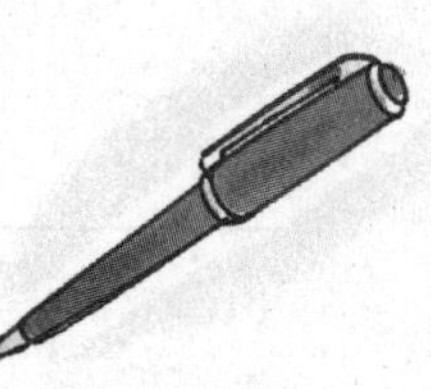

4. 

5. 

6. 

7. 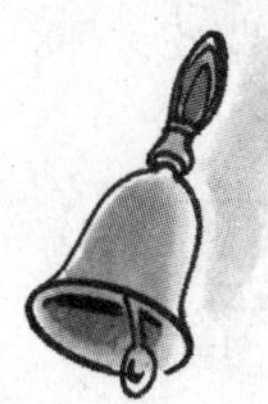

8. 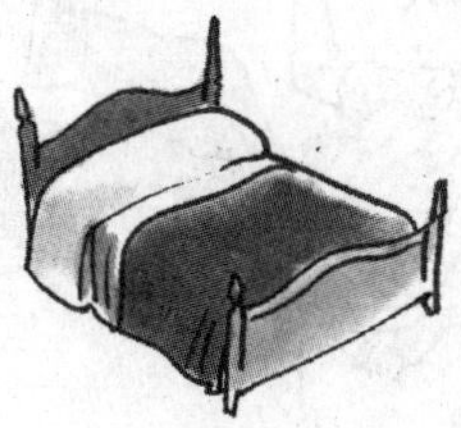

9. 

SCHOOL-HOME CONNECTION Use the words on this page to explore short vowel sounds. Substitute the *e* in each word with another vowel (*ten, tan*). Talk about the new words (or nonsense words) that are created.

Name ________________________________

▶ **Join the naming parts of the two sentences. Use the word <u>and</u>. Write the new sentence.**

1. Todd ran. His dog ran.

2. Todd fell down. His dog fell down.

TRY THIS

Write two sentences about something you and a friend do together. Use the word <u>and</u> to join the naming parts of the two sentences.

SCHOOL-HOME CONNECTION Encourage your child to tell you about sentences that have two naming parts. Together, say some sentences about two family members or friends.

Name ____________________

▶ **Look at each picture. Circle the word that completes the sentence. Then write the word.**

want went sent

1. Jeff ________ for a walk.

met bet bat

2. Jeff ________ Tess.

pit pat pet

3. Look at my little ________.

hem hen hint

4. It is a ________.

TRY THIS Write your own sentence with the word let. Draw a picture to go with your sentence.

SCHOOL-HOME CONNECTION Ask your child to name some words with short *e*. Have your child point out the *e* in words on this page.

Name ______________________

▶ **Read the words in the box. Write the word that best completes each sentence.**

was	her	said	with	every	day

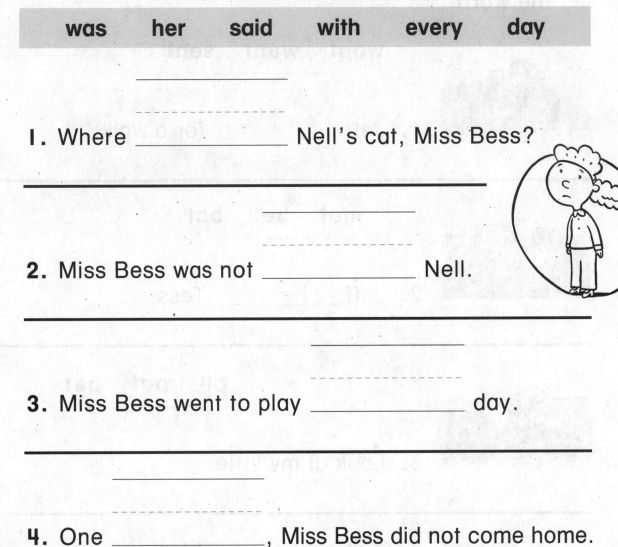

1. Where ____________ Nell's cat, Miss Bess?

2. Miss Bess was not ____________ Nell.

3. Miss Bess went to play ____________ day.

4. One ____________, Miss Bess did not come home.

5. "Dad, help me look for ____________," said Nell.

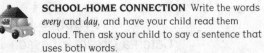

SCHOOL-HOME CONNECTION Write the words *every* and *day*, and have your child read them aloud. Then ask your child to say a sentence that uses both words.

Name ___

▶ **Write the word in the box that names each picture.**

sock bed vest pot fox neck doll net top

1.

2.

3.

4.

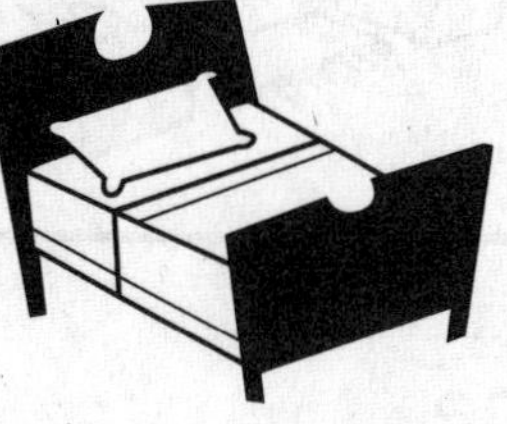

5.

6.

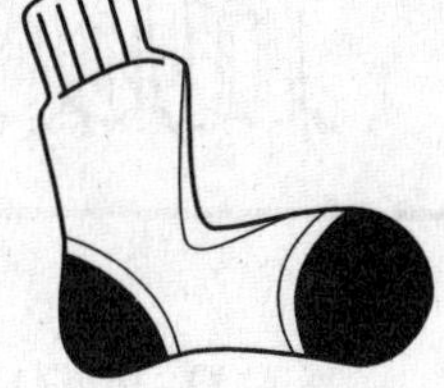

7.

8.

9.

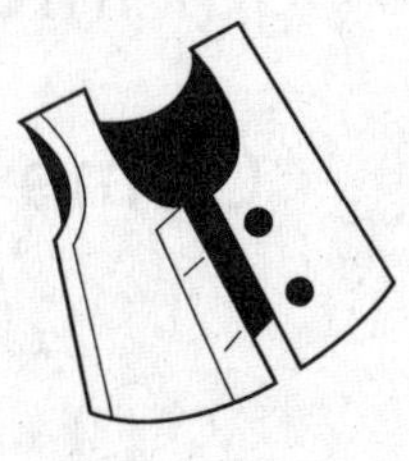

SCHOOL-HOME CONNECTION Ask your child to tell you about the pictures on this page. Together, think of some words that rhyme with *sock*.

Name ______________________________

Read each story beginning. Circle the picture that shows the story setting.

1. Deb and her dad walked up the hill.

   Deb said, "What a big hill! I want to get to the top. Don't you?"

   "Yes," said Dad. "We will walk and walk. We can get to the top."

2. Ken went into the pond. "Look at me,"

   Ken said, "I am all wet."

   Todd said, "I want to go in, too! I will get into the pond."

   "Come on!" said Ken.

SCHOOL-HOME CONNECTION With your child, talk about a favorite story. Ask your child what the story setting is.

Name ______________________________

▶ **Say each picture name. Listen to the beginning sounds. Write the two letters that stand for the beginning sounds.**

sk	sl	sn	sp	st

1. ______

2. ______

3. ______

4. ______

5. ______

6. ______

7. ______

8. ______

9. ______

SCHOOL-HOME CONNECTION Write the word *stop*, and let your child read it aloud. Then have your child make a red stop sign.

Name ______________________

▶ **Read the words. Then read the name of each group. Write each word in the group where it belongs.**

Words That Begin With th	Words That End With th

Words Without th

Spelling Words

then
them
this
that
path
with
men
set
was
said

SCHOOL-HOME CONNECTION Have your child read the Spelling Words aloud to you. Take turns making up sentences using the words.

Name ________________________________

▶ **Say each picture name. Write th if its name begins or ends with th.**

1.
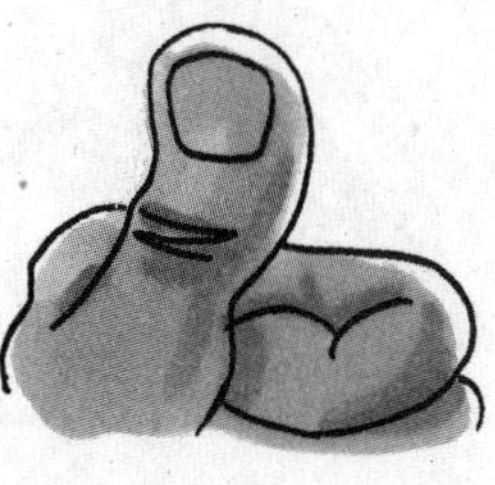

2.

3.
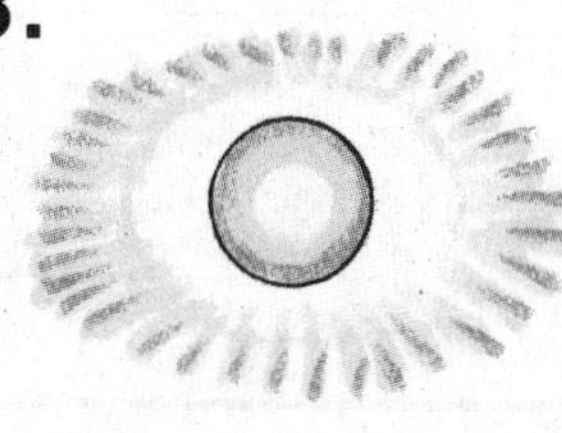

4.

5.
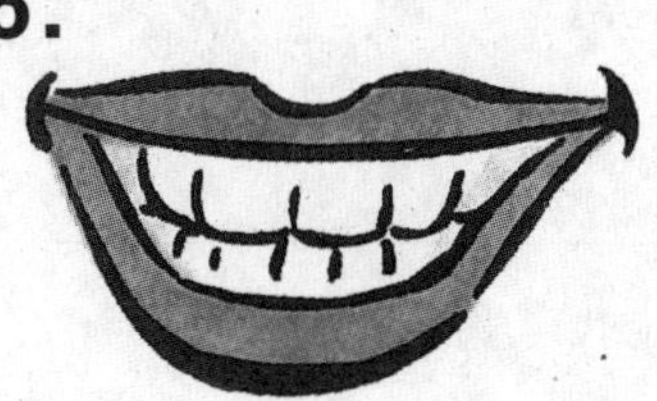

6.

7.

8.

9.
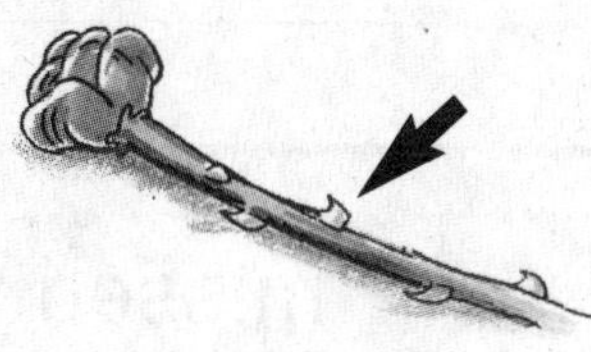

SCHOOL-HOME CONNECTION Sing together "Where Is Thumbkin?" Encourage your child to add motions by wiggling his or her thumbs as if they are talking to each other.

Name ______________________________

▶ Write the telling part of each sentence.

1. Zack slid.

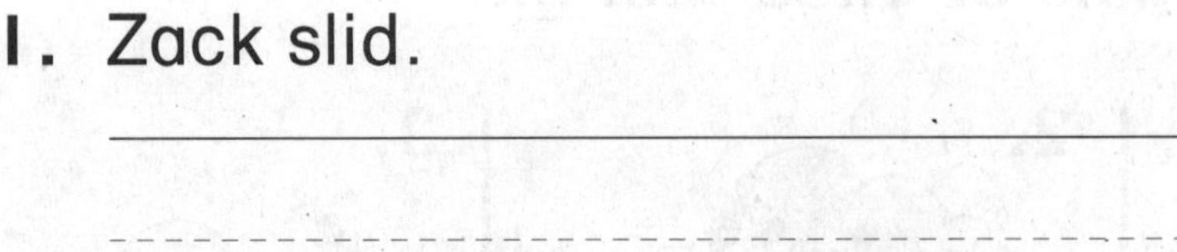

---

2. Zack looks.

---

3. He sees.

---

4. He calls.

---

5. I missed you, Mom.

SCHOOL-HOME CONNECTION Encourage your child to say several sentences telling what he or she likes to do at home. Together, talk about the telling parts of your child's sentences.

Name ____________________

▶ **Look at each picture. Write the word in the box that completes each sentence.**

This	**thin**	**path**	**moth**	**math**

1. The cat hops on the ________.

2. Tom is good at ________.

3. Hap looks too ________.

4. Can you see the ________?

5. ________ hat looks good on me.

SCHOOL-HOME CONNECTION Say the following words and ask your child to say a rhyming word that begins with the sound *th*: tank (thank), *hum* (thumb), *horn* (thorn), and *tick* (thick).

Name ______________________

▶ **Read the words in the box. Write the word that best completes each sentence.**

put	she	new	friends	use	could

1. Where did you ______________ my ball?

2. I want to ______________ it.

3. My new ______________ will come to play with me.

4. You ______________ toss the ball and let us run for it.

5. Did ______________ take my ball?

SCHOOL-HOME CONNECTION Write the word *friends* and let your child read it to you. Together, talk about what your child enjoys doing with friends.

Name ___________________

▶ **Look at each picture. Write the word in the box that completes each sentence.**

This	thin	path	moth	math

1. The cat hops on the ________.

2. Tom is good at ________.

3. Hap looks too ________.

4. Can you see the ________?

5. ________ hat looks good on me.

SCHOOL-HOME CONNECTION Say the following words and ask your child to say a rhyming word that begins with the sound *th*: tank (thank), *hum* (thumb), *horn* (thorn), and *tick* (thick).

Name ______________________________

▶ **Read the words in the box. Write the word that best completes each sentence.**

put	she	new	friends	use	could

1. Where did you ______________ my ball?

2. I want to ______________ it.

3. My new ______________ will come to play with me.

4. You ______________ toss the ball and let us run for it.

5. Did ______________ take my ball?

SCHOOL-HOME CONNECTION Write the word *friends* and let your child read it to you. Together, talk about what your child enjoys doing with friends.

Name ______________________

Phonics
CVCC-CCVC Words

▶ **Look at each picture. Write the word from the box that completes each sentence.**

slid	this	hill	with	that

1. "Look at __________ sled."

2. "We can go up this big __________."

3. They __________ down fast.

4. "Oh, I liked __________!"

5. "Can I go __________ you?"

SCHOOL-HOME CONNECTION Have your child read aloud the sentences he or she completed. Then ask your child to tell you a story about another sled ride.

Name ____________________

▶ **Look at each picture. Write the word from the box that completes the sentence.**

bent	best	tent	vest	west

1. Put on the __________.

2. Walk to the __________.

3. Pick up a __________ twig.

4. Help with the __________.

5. It's the __________!

SCHOOL-HOME CONNECTION Ask your child to read aloud some of the sentences he or she completed. Together, think of words that rhyme with *best*.

Name ___

▶ **Read the words. Then read the name of each group. Write each word in the group where it belongs.**

Words With u

Words Without u

Spelling Words

us
bus
bug
rug
mug
must
with
then
she
use

SCHOOL-HOME CONNECTION Ask your child to find Spelling Words that rhyme. Together, think of other words that rhyme with *bug*. Have your child make up a little poem using two of the rhyming words.

Name ______________________________

▶ **Write the word from the box that names each picture.**

bus	pup	sun	duck	cup	tusk	rug	tub	bug

1. 

2. 

3. 

4. 

5. 

6. 

7. 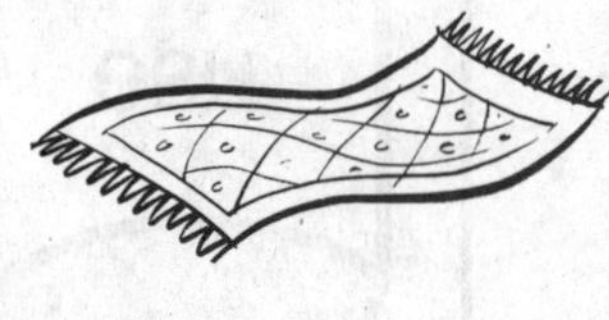

8. 

9. 

SCHOOL-HOME CONNECTION Ask your child to name some of the pictures on this page. Together, think of words that rhyme with *sun*.

Name ______________________

▶ **Use <u>and</u> to join the telling parts of the two sentences. Write the new sentence.**

1. Pam ran. Pam called the dog.

____

2. Tip got up. Tip ran.

____

Can you do two things at the same time? Write a sentence about what you can do. Draw a picture to go with it.

SCHOOL-HOME CONNECTION With your child, talk about outdoor activities your family enjoys. Use some sentences with telling parts for two things people do.

Name ______________________________

▶ **Write the word from the box that completes each sentence.**

truck	mud	fun	stump	hug	tub

1.

Pigs play in the ______________.

2.

The pup is in the ______________.

3.

Dad likes to ______________ him.

4.

The men pack the ______________.

5.

The friends had ______________.

6.

He jumped over the ______________.

SCHOOL-HOME CONNECTION Say a sentence with one incorrect word. Challenge your child to listen carefully, identify the word, and say the sentence correctly.

Name ______________________________

▶ **Write the word that best completes each sentence.**

he says your

1. Bud ____________ it is hot in here.

out oh of

2. "Let's go ____________," he says.

he your people

3. "We can go see ____________ friends."

When With Was

4. "____________ do you want to go?"

gives people night

5. "I don't like to go out at ____________."

SCHOOL-HOME CONNECTION Write the word *people* and have your child read it. Together, name some of the people you know.

Name ______________________________

Write the words where they belong in the puzzle.

cup	desk	duck	neck	nut	pen

1.

6.

2.

3.

4.

5.

2. ↓
1. →
4. ↓
3. →
6. ↓
5. →

SCHOOL-HOME CONNECTION Encourage your child to read aloud some of the words he or she wrote in the crossword puzzle. Together, talk about other kinds of puzzles you enjoy.

Name ______________________________

▶ **Name each picture. Listen to the beginning sounds. Write the two letters that stand for the beginning sounds.**

tr	cr	pr	dr	gr	fr

1. ______	**2.** ______	**3.** ______
4. ______	**5.** ______	**6.** ______
7. ______	**8.** ______	**9.** ______

SCHOOL-HOME CONNECTION Ask your child about the pictures on this page. Together, think of other words that begin with the sounds at the beginning of the word *train*.

Name ______________________________

▶ **Read the words. Then read the name of each group. Write each word in the group where it belongs.**

Words With ing | **Words With ang**

Words Without ng

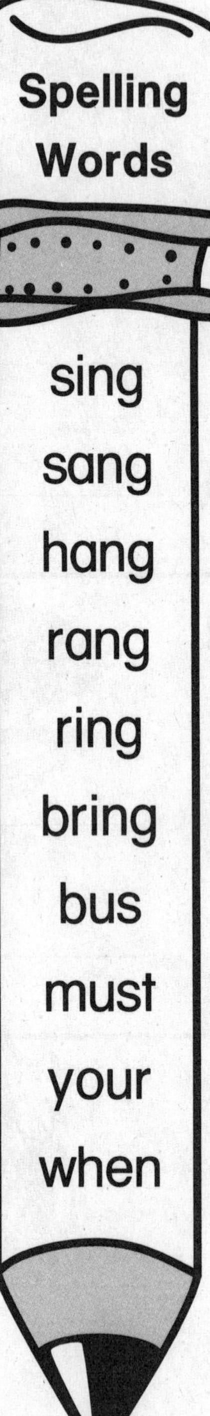

Spelling Words
sing
sang
hang
rang
ring
bring
bus
must
your
when

SCHOOL-HOME CONNECTION Have your child read the Spelling Words aloud to you. Then ask your child to find pairs of Spelling Words that are the same except for one letter. (*sing, sang*); (*rang, ring*)

Name ___________________________

▶ **Say each picture name. Color the picture if its name has the sound /ng/.**

1.

2.

3.

4.

5.

6.

7.

8.

9.

SCHOOL-HOME CONNECTION Have your child name the pictures he or she colored. Take turns saying words that rhyme with *ring*.

Name ______________________

▶ **Complete each sentence. Write either a naming part or a telling part.**

1. Dogs ______________________.

2. ______________________ can hop.

3. My friends ______________________.

4. ______________________ played.

5. ______________________ is happy.

TRY THIS What can you do? Write a complete sentence that tells about it. If you like, draw a picture to go with your sentence.

SCHOOL-HOME CONNECTION Ask your child to say a complete sentence that tells something he or she did today. Encourage your child to write the sentence.

Name ___________________________

▶ **Look at each picture. Write the word from the box that completes the clue.**

king	long	ring	sing	wings

1. I can ____________.

2. I am ____________.

3. I am for a ____________.

4. I have ____________.

5. I can ____________.

SCHOOL-HOME CONNECTION Have your child read aloud the sentences he or she completed. Then take turns giving riddle clues about words that end in *ng*.

Name ______________________

Write the word from the box that completes each sentence.

from	eat	or	grows	two	gone

1. What can we ____________?

2. The best things are ____________!

3. I see ____________ cans here.

4. We can eat that ____________ go out.

5. We could get a snack ____________ Ted.

6. He ____________ the best things to eat!

SCHOOL-HOME CONNECTION With your child, talk about foods your family likes to eat. Ask your child to help you prepare a snack or a meal.

Name ___________________________________

▶ **Read each sentence. Add to the picture.**

1.

Add a stack of bricks.

2.

Add a bug that can sting.

3.

Add two things to bring.

4.

Add a snack for the kids.

SCHOOL-HOME CONNECTION Encourage your child to talk about what he or she has drawn. Ask your child how he or she knew what to draw.

Name ______________________

▶ **Read about the dog. Then write three details about the dog.**

We have a dog. We call her Brass. Brass is long, but she has little legs. We like to pet Brass. She likes it too. Brass can run fast on her little legs. I like to run with her. We all have fun with Brass!

____

____

____

SCHOOL-HOME CONNECTION Ask your child to tell you about the dog Brass. Together, talk about other kinds of pets.

Name ____________________

▶ **Complete each sentence. Write the contraction for the two words above the line.**

do not

1. I ____________ like going up.

It is

2. ____________ fun for me.

I will

3. ____________ go now and you can come next.

is not

4. It ____________ too tall.

You will

5. ____________ like it at the top.

SCHOOL-HOME CONNECTION Ask your child to point out one of the contractions he or she wrote. Then have your child identify the two words that are combined in that contraction.

Name ________________________________

▶ **Read the words. Then read the name of each group. Write each word in the group where it belongs.**

Words With or	Words Without or

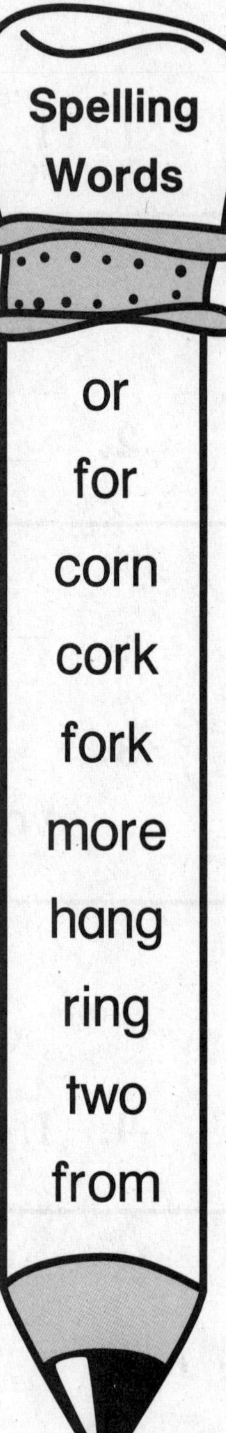

Spelling Words
or
for
corn
cork
fork
more
hang
ring
two
from

SCHOOL-HOME CONNECTION Have your child read the Spelling Words to you. Ask which three Spelling Words rhyme. (*or, for, more*) Together, think of other words that rhyme with *or*.

Name ______________________________

Write the word from the box that names each picture.

fort	corn	store	horn	fork	score

1. ______________

2. ______________

3. ______________

4. ______________

5. ______________

6. ______________

TRY THIS! Write your own sentence with the word or. Draw a picture to go with your sentence.

SCHOOL-HOME CONNECTION Ask your child to write the word *or*. Then have your child say several other words that contain the *or* sound.

Name ___________________________

▶ **Read both words above each line. Choose the naming word that best completes the sentence.**

friend fork

1. I play with my ____________.

snacks socks

2. We eat ____________ first.

bill ball

3. Then we toss the ____________.

can crab

4. We look for a big ____________.

SCHOOL-HOME CONNECTION Let your child share what he or she learned about nouns. Then ask your child to say the naming words (nouns) for various people and things in your home.

Name ______________________________

▶ **Finish the story. Write the word from the box that completes each sentence.**

Mort	for	store	corn	born	more

A New Pig

"This is my pig," said Bob. "I call him

______________. He was little when he was

______________," said Bob.

"I like Mort," said Ann. "What is he eating?"

"That is ______________," Bob said. "It is good

______________ pigs. Let's go to the ______________

and get ______________."

SCHOOL-HOME CONNECTION Ask your child to write the word *born*. Discuss the date on which he or she was born.

Name ___

▶ **Write the word that best completes each sentence.**

time need saw

1. It's ___ for us to go out and act.

our right night

2. Do we look all ___, Mr. Dunn?

oh or our

3. We will do ___ best.

try time right

4. We'll ___ to do a good job.

the be Mr.

5. This will ___ fun!

SCHOOL-HOME CONNECTION Write the word *time* and have your child read it. Then take turns asking what times the members of your family do certain things.

Name ____________________

Write the words where they belong in the puzzles.

corn	horn	fork	cork	fort

1.

2.

3.

4.

5.

2. ↓

1. →

4. ↓

3. →

5. →

SCHOOL-HOME CONNECTION Ask your child to name some of the pictures on the page. Together, look for rhyming words in the cross-word puzzle.

Name ______________________

Read the story beginning. Then answer the questions about the characters.

Gus likes to play his drums. If Gus hasn't got his drums, he taps on things. Gus taps on cans. He taps on cups. He taps on mugs. He taps on desks and beds.

"Stop!" says Mom.

"No more!" says Dad.

"Do not tap!" says Ben.

"Oh-oh!" says little Peg.

Gus nods and says, "O.K." He puts his drum sticks down.

In no time, Gus picks the sticks back up. Tap, tap, tap. Gus taps all the time.

1. Who is the main character?

____

2. Name two more story characters.

______________________ ______________________

SCHOOL-HOME CONNECTION Ask your child to tell you about the story character Gus. Then encourage your child to tell you an original story about Gus.

Name ______________________

Write a compound word to name each picture. Use a word from the first box and a word from the second box to make each compound word.

ant	back	pop
sand	sun	wind

box	corn	hill
mill	pack	set

1. 

____

2. 

____

3. 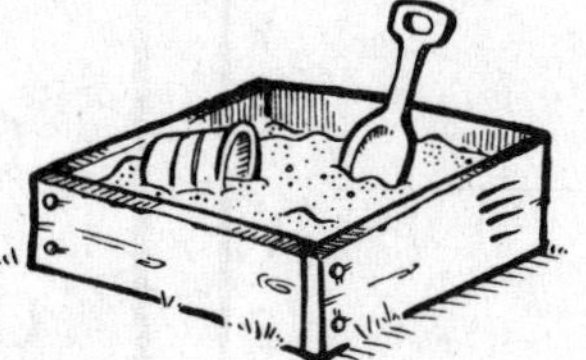

____

4. 

____

5. 

____

6. 

____

SCHOOL-HOME CONNECTION Have your child read aloud the words he or she wrote to name the pictures on this page. Ask what two words make up each compound word.

Name ______________________

▶ **Read the words. Then read the name of each group. Write each word in the group where it belongs.**

Words That Begin With sh	**Words That End With sh**

Words Without sh

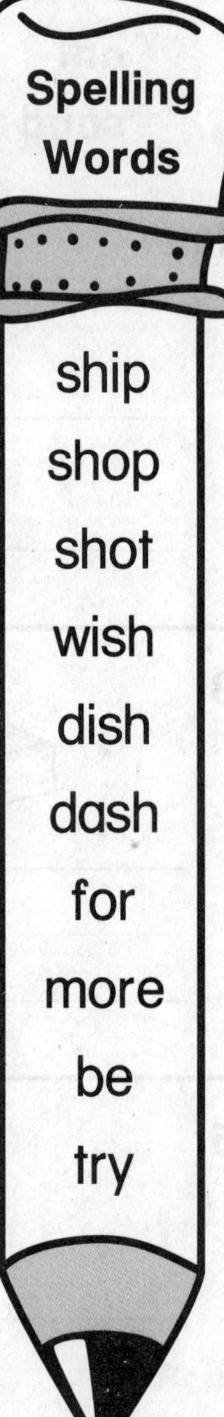

Spelling
Words
ship
shop
shot
wish
dish
dash
for
more
be
try

SCHOOL-HOME CONNECTION Ask your child to read the Spelling Words aloud to you. Then take turns making up sentences using two or three of the words.

Name ______________________

Write the word from the box that names each picture.

dish	ship	flash	shop	fish	shack

1. ______________________

2. ______________________

3. ______________________

4. ______________________

5. ______________________

6. ______________________

TRY THIS Finish this sentence: I wish ______________________.
Draw a picture to go with your sentence.

SCHOOL-HOME CONNECTION Ask your child to write the word *fish*. Then have your child say several other words that include the /sh/ sound.

Name ______________________

Write the words in each sentence that name a person or a place.

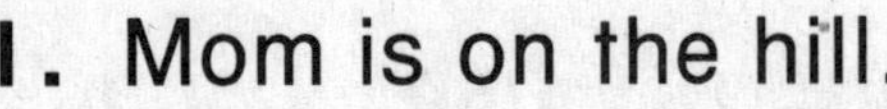

1. Mom is on the hill.

2. Dad walks to the pond.

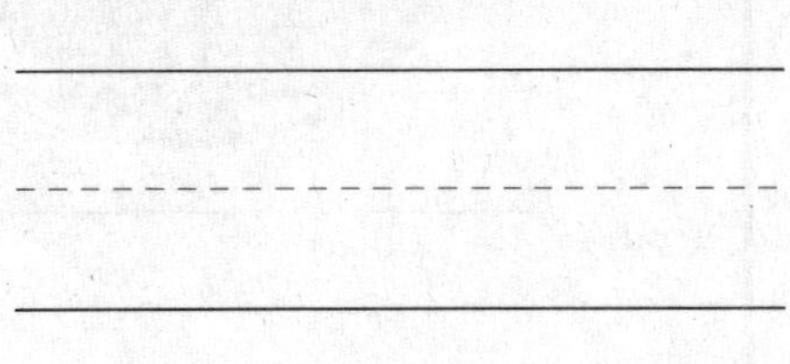

3. The friend has a doll.

4. The man went to the store.

5. The kids look at the tadpoles.

SCHOOL-HOME CONNECTION Ask your child to tell you about nouns that name places. Together, name places where your child likes to spend time.

Name ____________________

▶ Look at the pictures. Circle the word that completes the sentence. Then write the word.

swim win fish

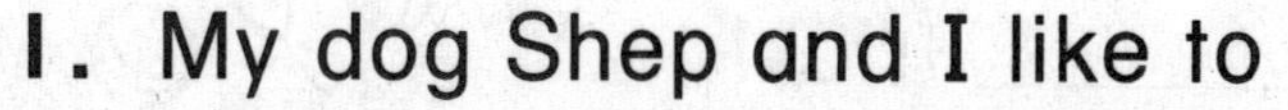

1. My dog Shep and I like to ________.

ship shop shin

2. We see a big ________.

more shore ship

3. We run on the ________.

dish dock shop

4. Shep can drink from a ________.

rash rush brush

5. Then I ________ Shep.

SCHOOL-HOME CONNECTION Ask your child to read the words he or she added to the sentences. Have your child tell what two letters stand for the /sh/ sound.

Name ______________________

▶ **Circle and write the word that best completes each sentence.**

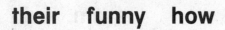

their funny how

1. That is a ________ trick!

hide away many

2. How ________ balls do you see?

How Some Hide

3. ________ can they do that?

how away some

4. Now they want ________ snacks.

from food fell

5. She has ________ for them.

SCHOOL-HOME CONNECTION Have your child read aloud one of the sentences he or she completed. Then ask your child to make up a different sentence using the word he or she wrote.

Name ___________________________________

▶ **Look at each picture. Write the word from the box that completes the sentence.**

ship	fish	wish	shed	dish

1. I ____________ I had a cat.

2. I wish I had a ____________.

3. I wish I had a ____________.

4. I wish I had a ____________.

5. I wish I had a ____________.

SCHOOL-HOME CONNECTION Have your child read aloud some of the sentences he or she completed. Then take turns finishing this sentence: I *wish* _____.

Name ______________________________

Read about the bug. Then write three details about it.

Look at this bug! It is very big. It is red with black spots. It has six long legs. It has wings, too. It landed on my hand. I got to look at it for a long time. I like this bug.

SCHOOL-HOME CONNECTION Ask your child to read aloud the paragraph on this page. Together, talk about real bugs your child has seen.

Name ______________________________

Look at each picture. Circle the word that completes the sentence. Then write the word.

1. My horse will ____________.

still
trot
trick

---

2. We can ____________ here.

grow
stop
skip

---

3. Can we ____________ here?

crank
from
cross

4. The horses want to ____________.

spill
drink
drip

Where would you like to go? Write your own sentence with the word trip. Draw a picture to go with your sentence.

SCHOOL-HOME CONNECTION Have your child read aloud one of the words he or she wrote on this page. Ask your child to say other words that begin with the same pair of letters as that word.

"It was not my day!"
said Fox.

8

Fold

Fix-It Fox

1

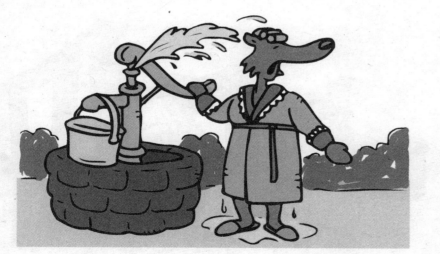

"Fox!" said Peg. "Help
me with the well!"

6

Fold

"Yes, my pet," said Fox.

3

"Fox!" yelled Peg.
"The leg fell off.
Will you fix the bed?"

2

"Here I come, Peg!" said Fox.

7

Fold

"Fox," said Peg. "Every
day we see that mess.
Can you fix it?"

4

"You bet!" Fox called to her.

5

Fold

8 Here he is! That Ben!

1

Fold

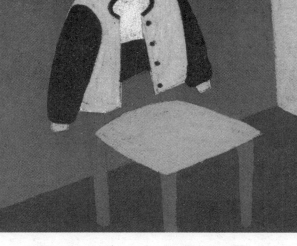

6 Where could Ben go?

He put his new boots here. 3

Fold

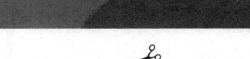

2 Mom looks for Ben.

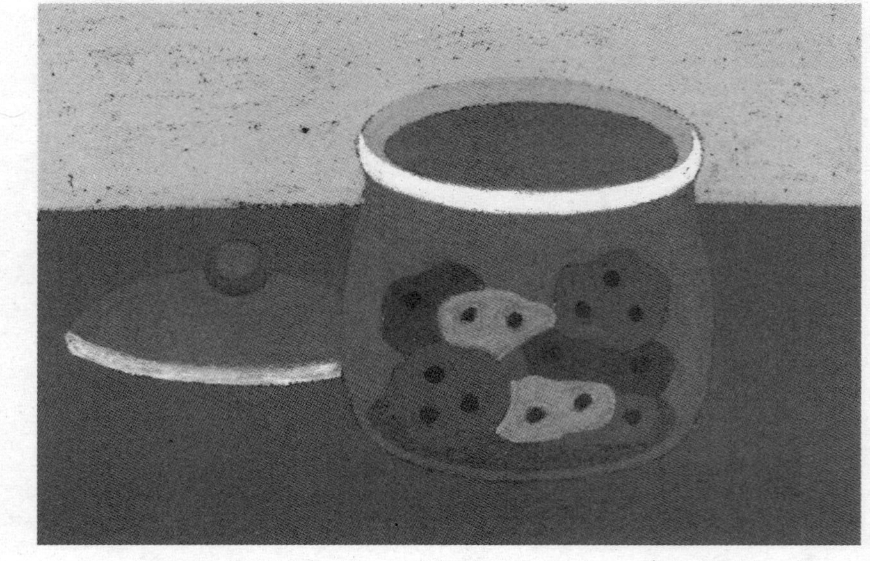

Is Ben here with his friends? 7

Fold

4 Then he left his cap on a peg.

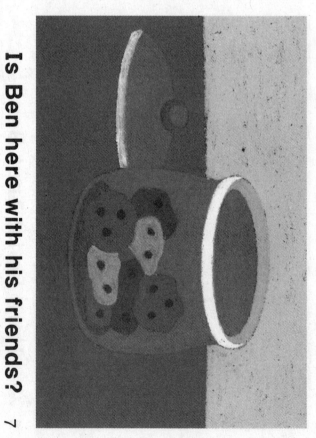

She sees a backpack.

Did Ben use this? 5

Do You See It?

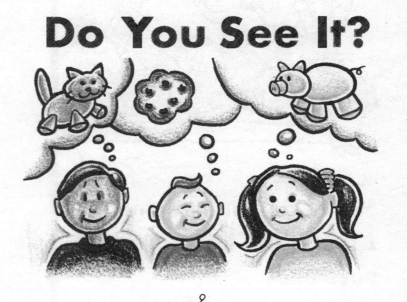

1

"I'll help you hunt," says Seth.
"I see your pig up here." 3

"Now my cat is missing,"
says Seth.
6 "We can all hunt for it," says Max.

"Thanks, people!
8 Now we all have what we want."

Fold

Fold

"Seth, do you see my pig?
I had it out last night,"
2 says Jess.

Fold

"I see your cat, Seth," says Jess.
"It's up on top." 7

"I want my snack," says Max.
4 "When did that dog get it?"

Fold

"I'll get it for you," says Seth.
He gives the snack to Max. 5

Frank from Moss Pond

1

Frank hops to where the tall
plant grows.
He has lots of bugs to eat. 3

One night, they sang a
long song.

6

When the night was gone,
so was the song.

8

Fold

Fold

Frank is a frog from Moss Pond.
2 He can hop from rock to rock.

The frogs sang and sang.
The song ended with a bang! 7

Fold

4 At night, Frank sings songs
with his friends.

They like to sing one or
two songs every night. 5

Just One More

1

"Mom, I need just one more." 3

"This is our last one. Then
you'll go right to bed." 6

"It's time for a
good-night kiss!" 8

Fold

Fold

This is a good snack.

2 I will try just one more.

"This is good! I want just

one more thing, Mom." 7

Fold

"Here's one more for you.

4 Then it will be time for bed."

"I saw one more, Mom.

Can I have it?" 5

Fold

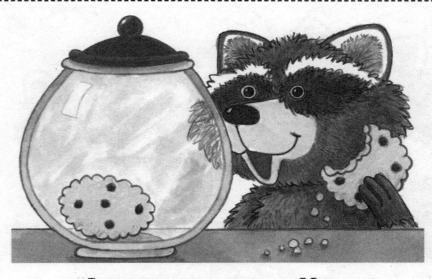

Travis and his fish are home.
8 How many fish do you see?

At the Fish Shop

1

Fold

Dad gets fish food from the shelf.
Travis looks at the fish. Some fish
6 look back at him. Some swim away.

Travis and Dad pick out a fish tank.
They will need many things for
their fish. 3

Fold

Travis and his dad are going to the fish shop.

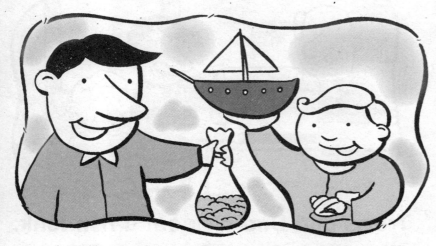

2

Travis picks his fish. He picks one funny fish. Now he and his dad have all they need.

7

Fold

Some rocks and shells will look grand. Here is a ship.

4

They'll need plants. Their fish can hide in them.

5

Fold

TROPHIES

Level Three

Here and There

Name ______________________________

▶ **Read the words. Then read the name of each group. Write each word in the group where it belongs.**

Words With ch

______________ | ______________

______________ | ______________

______________ | ______________

______________ | ______________

______________ | ______________

Words With sh

______________ | ______________

______________ | ______________

Words Without ch or sh

______________ | ______________

______________ | ______________

Spelling
Words
chip
chin
inch
itch
catch
match
wish
shop
how
many

SCHOOL-HOME CONNECTION Point to and read the Spelling Words aloud with your child. Talk about what is the same and what is different about the words.

Name ______________________

▶ **Circle the word that best completes the sentence. Then write the word.**

stick
thick
chick

1. The ______________ rips his red hat.

---

fat
fetch
fish

2. Mom Hen tells him to ______________ the pins.

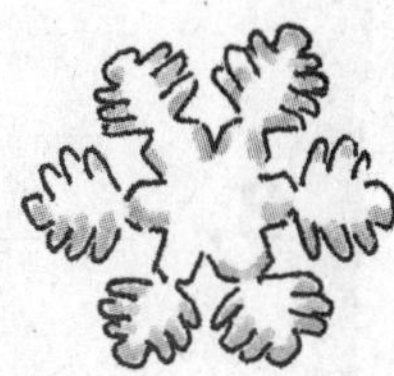

---

patch
match
catch

3. Mom Hen can fix the rip with a ______________.

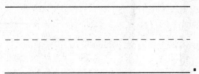

stiff
stitch
snatch

4. Mom Hen will ______________ it on.

---

chip
hill
chill

5. The chick will not get a ______________.

SCHOOL-HOME CONNECTION Chat with your child about how to dress in chilly weather.

Name ______________________

▶ **In the barn, write the words that name animals. In the house, write the words that name things.**

hen	lamp	bed	pig	milk	cat	horse	car

1. ______________________

2. ______________________

3. ______________________

4. ______________________

5. ______________________

6. ______________________

7. ______________________

8. ______________________

TRY THIS Draw a picture of an animal you like. Label your picture.

SCHOOL-HOME CONNECTION Look through a photo album or magazine with your child. Name each thing or animal you see.

Name ___________________________________

▶ **Circle the sentence that tells about each picture.**

1. Chip likes to chop the ball.
Chip likes to pitch the ball.
Chip likes to sketch the ball.

2. Rich can not catch the ball.
Rich can catch the ball.
Rich chats with Chip.

3. The friends play hopscotch.
The friends hop in the ditch.
The friends sit on a bench.

4. Wag can hatch a chick.
Wag can get on the branch.
Wag can fetch the stick.

5. Chet is the champ.
Chet chomps on an apple.
Chet checks the chimp.

SCHOOL-HOME CONNECTION Watch part of a sports game together. Talk about the rules. Ask your child to draw a picture of a sports champion.

Name ___________________________

▶ **Write the word that best completes each sentence.**

animals air act

1. What is that fluff in the ____________?

live last leg

2. Lots of hens ____________ here.

fly eat live

3. Hens cannot ____________.

taps turns yells

4. The hen ____________ around in the nest.

around much soon

5. The eggs will hatch ____________.

SCHOOL-HOME CONNECTION Have your child write the words *air, around, live, animals, soon, fly,* and *turns* on separate slips of paper. Put them face down on a table. Take turns selecting words and using them in sentences.

Name ________________________________

Circle the sentence that tells about each picture.

1. Chad can chop the ball.
   Chad can pitch the ball.
   Chad can sketch the ball.

2. Will Ellen catch the ball?
   Will Ellen cash the ball?
   Will Ellen flash the ball?

3. Patch will sit on the bench.
   Patch will hop in a ditch.
   Patch has an itch.

4. Chet stops to chat.
   Chet picks up a watch.
   Chet picks up shells.

5. Beth will dash to catch Chum.
   Beth will go to a shop.
   Beth will get on a branch.

Draw a picture to show something that you like to do.

SCHOOL-HOME CONNECTION Ask your child to read aloud the sentences she or he circled. Discuss how your child decided which ones to circle.

Name ______________________________

▶ **Write <u>cl</u>, <u>fl</u>, or <u>pl</u> to complete each word.**

1. Milt can do a __________ip.

2. Milt has a __________ant.

3. A __________ag pops out.

4. It's a __________ock.

5. We grin and __________ap.

TRY THIS Draw a clown doing a funny trick. Write a title for your picture.

SCHOOL-HOME CONNECTION Ask your child to read the sentences to you. Work together to think of more words that begin with the same sounds as *plant*, *flag*, and *clock*.

Name ______________________

▶ **Read the words. Then read the name of each group. Write each word in the group where it belongs.**

Words With ar	**Words With n**
______	______
______	______
______	______
______	______
______	**Words With i**
______	______
______	______
______	______
______	______

Spelling Words
far
farm
arm
art
cart
card
chin
inch
live
soon

SCHOOL-HOME CONNECTION With your child, take turns saying sentences with a word missing. Complete each other's sentences with one of the Spelling Words.

Name ______________________

▶ **Name each picture. Write ar if the name has ar in it.**

1. c______

2. c______d

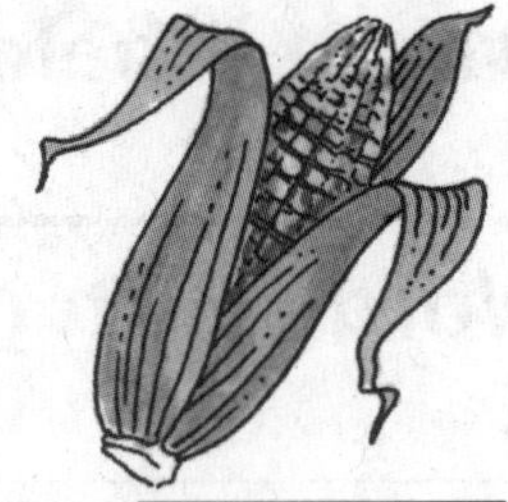

3. c______n

4. sc______f

5. h______se

6. h______p

7. h______n

8. st______

9. b______n

TRY THIS Make a card to give to a friend or family member.

SCHOOL-HOME CONNECTION The next time you take a ride in a car, make a game of thinking of as many *ar* words as you can.

Name ____________________

▶ **Write the word that best completes each sentence.**

pet pets

1. Chuck has six ______________.

dog dogs

2. One of the ______________ is small.

spot spots

3. The cat has a tan ______________.

snack snacks

4. Do the pets like ______________?

stick sticks

5. Champ runs to get a ______________.

SCHOOL-HOME CONNECTION Write a list of animals, some singular and some plural, such as *dog, cats, lions, tiger, ant, birds.* Ask your child which words name more than one.

Name ________________________________

▶ **Read the word. Circle the pictures whose names have the same vowel sound.**

1. start  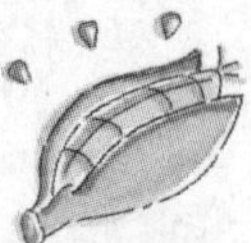

2. dark   

3. hard   

▶ **Read the sentences. Write the word that best completes each one.**

farm for

4. The ____________ is small.

barn bark

5. The horse snorts in the ____________.

card car

6. The dog barks at the ____________.

SCHOOL-HOME CONNECTION Talk with your child about the jobs of people you know. Discuss when people start their work day.

Name ____________________

▶ **Write the word that best completes each sentence.**

sometimes	take	there	city	house

1. Mr. Martin lives in the ________.

2. He has a brick ________.

3. He likes to ________ his dog to the park.

4. We ________ go to visit him.

5. It's not hard to get ________.

SCHOOL-HOME CONNECTION Ask your child to draw a picture of a city. Then ask her or him to write a sentence about the picture. Have your child use the word *city* in the sentence.

Name ____________________

▶ **Circle the word that names the picture.**
Then write the word.

1. park / port / play	2. star / hard / car	3. yard / fort / far
4. cart / jar / corn	**5.** farm / arm / corn	**6.** tar / form / card
7. horn / cord / art	**8.** yarn / corn / yard	**9.** harp / harm / horn

SCHOOL-HOME CONNECTION Ask your child to say each picture name. Then have him or her tell you which words have the sound /är/ as in *art*.

Name ______________________________

▶ **Read the story beginning. Then circle the picture that shows where the story takes place.**

Here we are! Look at all the cars and trucks! Let's stop at the hot dog stand. We can sit on a bench in the park. Watch for cars before you cross! The bus stop is not far from here.

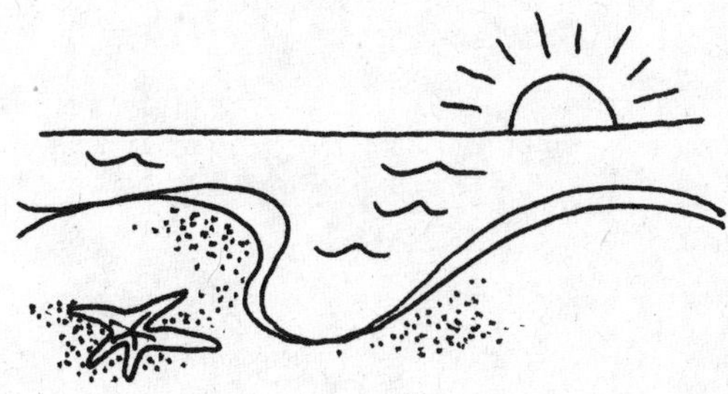

TRY THIS Think of another picture setting. Write about it.

SCHOOL-HOME CONNECTION Look at the pictures with your child. Talk about a story that might happen in each place.

Name ____________________

▶ **Finish each sentence. Put together the word and the word ending above the line. Write the new word.**

look + s

1. Nick ____________ at all the stars.

wish + ed

2. Nick ____________ for a star.

fish + ing

3. "I am ____________ for a star for you," said Nick's dad.

TRY THIS Write your own sentence about Nick. Use the word yell, and add the ending ed.

SCHOOL-HOME CONNECTION Ask your child to choose one of the sentences on this page and read it aloud. Discuss the ending added to the verb.

Name ______________________________

▶ **Read the words. Then read the name of each group. Write each word in the group where it belongs.**

Words With <u>qu</u>	**Words With <u>wh</u>**
______________	______________
______________	______________
______________	______________
	______________
	______________
Words With <u>ar</u>	**Words With <u>e</u>**
______________	______________
______________	______________
______________	______________

Spelling Words

quit
quick
quiz
whiz
which
when
arm
card
who
there

SCHOOL-HOME CONNECTION Point to the Spelling Words. Have your child read them to you. Help your child think of other words with the same beginning or ending sound.

Name ______________________________

▶ **Write the word that best completes each sentence.**

quilt quack quit

1. When did Jen get this ______________?

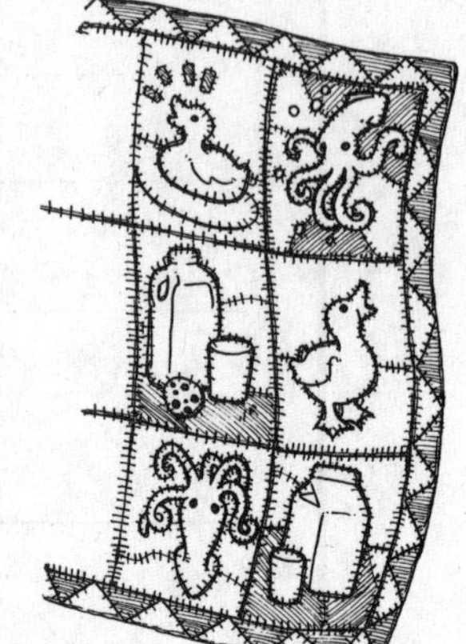

When Which Will

2. ______________ quilt is it?

squid squint quit

3. Jen's quilt has a pink ______________ on it.

Whip Wig What

4. ______________ is that by the squid?

quitting quizzing quacking

5. It looks like a ______________ duck.

SCHOOL-HOME CONNECTION Ask your child to read aloud some of the sentences. Have your child say a new sentence using a word that he or she didn't use on the page.

Name ______________________________

Read the names. Write the special names and titles correctly.

1. janet sanchez ______________________________

2. uncle chuck ______________________________

3. mrs. dunn ______________________________

4. dr. fitch ______________________________

5. marcus ______________________________

6. mr. york ______________________________

SCHOOL-HOME CONNECTION Help your child make a list of people he or she knows. Have him or her make sure all the names and titles begin with a capital letter.

Name ____________________

Phonics

Digraphs: /kw/qu, /hw/wh

▶ **Circle the word that completes the sentence. Then write the word.**

What
Where
Whack

1. ____________ is that song?

Quick
Quilt
Quart

2. It's called "The ____________ Step."

Whiz
Whip
Which

3. ____________ song do you like more, "The Quick Step" or "Squish, Squish"?

When
Quilt
Whip

4. ____________ will the band start playing?

Quiz
Quit
Quart

5. The song I like best is "____________ That Quacking!"

SCHOOL-HOME CONNECTION Ask your child to help you make up silly lyrics for one of the song titles in the activity. Try to use words with *wh* and *qu*.

Name ______________________

▶ **Write the word that best completes each sentence.**

frost family book

1. Tim's ______________ likes to read to him.

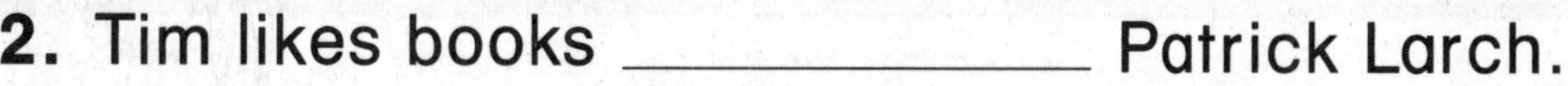

at to by

2. Tim likes books ______________ Patrick Larch.

grew buy good

3. Fran ______________ to like books about quilts.

by about for

4. Kim is reading many books ______________ ants.

writing sandwich wasn't

5. Reading and ______________ are fun, but I work hard, too.

SCHOOL-HOME CONNECTION Ask your child to talk about his or her favorite book. Why does your child like the book?

Name ____________________

Write the word from the box that completes each sentence.

Wham	Quack	Which	Quick	When

1. ____________ will the band come?

2. ____________! I can see them marching.

3. ____________! The drums come marching past.

4. ____________ one is Dennis?

5. "____________," went the ducks.

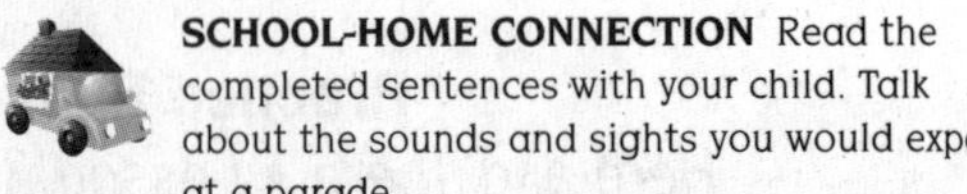

SCHOOL-HOME CONNECTION Read the completed sentences with your child. Talk about the sounds and sights you would expect at a parade.

Name ____________________

Read the story. Then answer the questions.

Cat was hunting for food. Just then Ant yelled for help. Cat looked until she saw Ant. He was swimming in milk!

"Help me!" said Ant. "I can't get out!"

"I'll help," said Cat. "I like milk!" So Cat licked up the milk.

"Thank you!" said Ant.

Dog saw what had happened.

Dog said, "Cat helped Ant, but Ant helped Cat, too."

1. Who are the main characters in the story?

____

2. Who else is in the story?

____

SCHOOL-HOME CONNECTION Ask your child to read the story aloud to you. Talk about the characters.

Name ______________________

▶ Write the word from the box that names each picture.

blocks	clap	flag	plant	flip	sled

1. ______________

2. ______________

3. ______________

4. ______________

5. ______________

6. ______________

SCHOOL-HOME CONNECTION Ask your child to choose one of the pictures on this page and read the word that names the picture. Together, think of other words that begin with the same sounds.

Name ______________________

▶ **Read the words. Then read the name of each group. Write each word in the group where it belongs.**

Words With ir

____

____

____

Words With ur

____

____

Words Without ir or ur

____

____

____

____

____

Spelling Words

sir
dirt
bird
burn
fur
her
quit
when
work
grew

SCHOOL-HOME CONNECTION Point to and read the Spelling Words with your child. Help your child think of words that rhyme with each word.

Name ____________________

▶ **Write the word from the box that best completes each sentence.**

her	fur	girl	purr	bird

1. The ____________ stands still.

2. She sees a little ____________.

3. Here comes ____________ cat.

4. She pats the cat's ____________.

5. The cat starts to ____________.

SCHOOL-HOME CONNECTION Ask your child to read aloud the words in the box. Together, think of other words that contain the /ûr/ sound.

Name ____________________

▶ **Read each sentence. Circle the special name of a place. Then write that special name correctly.**

1. We like to walk up cactus hill.

2. Who got wet in lock pond?

3. It's fun to play in rock park.

4. We can eat at Mrs. Pitt's snack shop.

TRY THIS Write the special name of a place you like to visit. Draw a picture of that place, too.

SCHOOL-HOME CONNECTION Let your child read aloud one of the special place names. Then help your child think of the special names of other places.

Name ___

Write the word from the box that best completes each sentence.

first	chirp	birds	ever	turns

1. Four ___ are standing here.
2. They will take ___.
3. The ___ one is by the birdbath.
4. Will she ___ fly away?
5. The birds start to ___.

TRY THIS Write your own sentence about being first. Draw a picture to go with your sentence.

SCHOOL-HOME CONNECTION Encourage your child to suggest words that rhyme with *her*.

Name ______________________

▶ **Write the word from the box that best completes each sentence.**

four find found full follow these way were

1. There were __________ girls at the park.

2. The first girl __________ food in her pocket.

3. Girls were eating until they were __________.

4. __________ two big kids want to find the girls.

5. Which __________ did they go? Let's follow them.

SCHOOL-HOME CONNECTION Write the words from the box on a piece of paper. As you point to each word, ask your child to read it, then use it in a sentence.

Name ______________________________

▶ **Circle the word that completes each sentence. Then write the word.**

hut hurt

1. Look at the little ____________.

bun burn

2. Don't get a sun ____________!

chip chirp

3. The bird gives a ____________.

cub curb

4. Step up on the ____________.

her herd

5. It looks like a big ____________.

SCHOOL-HOME CONNECTION Ask your child to read aloud some of the sentences on the page. Talk about the word choices above each blank. Ask what is different about each pair of words.

Name ______________________________

▶ **Read the story. Then circle the picture that shows where the story happened.**

"Let's play catch!" said Bert.

"It's too wet to go out," said Bess. "Let's play checkers."

"Let's ask Kurt to visit," said Bert. "Then we can play cards."

So they called Kurt and asked him to play cards.

Kurt said, "The sun is out now. Let's play catch!"

SCHOOL-HOME CONNECTION Ask your child to draw a picture of a place where he or she likes to play. Then have your child tell a story that could happen in the setting she or he drew.

Name ______________________________

▶ **Put together the word and the word ending above the lines. Write the new word to complete the sentence.**

purr + ing

1. The cat was ______________ in the girl's lap.

bark + ed

2. The dog ______________.

chirp + ed

3. Then a bird ______________.

want + s

4. Now the cat ______________ to go out.

SCHOOL-HOME CONNECTION Ask your child to read aloud the words he or she wrote. Discuss the word endings.

Name ______________________________

▶ **Read the words. Then read the name of each group. Write each word in the group where it belongs.**

Words With dd	**Words With r**
______________	______________
______________	______________
______________	______________
______________	______________

Words With gg

______________	______________

Spelling Words

middle
fiddle
wiggle
giggle
puddle
cuddle
fur
bird
were
four

SCHOOL-HOME CONNECTION Point to and read the Spelling Words with your child. Discuss how the words are alike and how they are different.

Name ______________________________

▶ **Write the word from the box that names each picture.**

candle	rattle	pickle	apple	bottle	kettle

1.

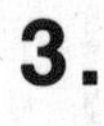

2.

3.

4.

5.

6.

SCHOOL-HOME CONNECTION Say these words that end in *le*: *wiggle, giggle, cackle, paddle, tickle.* Let your child act out the words.

Name ______________________________

▶ **Read each sentence. Circle the name of the day. Then write the name correctly.**

1. On monday we fed the pigs.

2. We fed the ducks on wednesday.

3. We walked the horses on thursday.

4. On friday we rest! ______________________________

TRY THIS! Write a sentence about your favorite day of the week. Use the name of the day in your sentence.

SCHOOL-HOME CONNECTION With your child, use a calendar to review the names of the days of the week.

Name ____________________

▶ **Read the riddles. Choose the best answer and write it on the line.**

1. Ducks do it when they walk.
Is it **waddle**, **rattle**, or **wall**?

2. You do it if you are glad.
Is it **giggle**, **good**, or **grill**?

3. It is not big.
Is it **let**, **kettle**, or **little**?

4. It makes a good snack.
Is it **middle**, **apple**, or **puddle**?

5. You can make something to eat in it.
Is it **cackle**, **kettle**, or **kid**?

6. You can put this in a sandwich.
Is it **purple**, **pickle**, or **pimple**?

SCHOOL-HOME CONNECTION Ask your child to read each riddle to family members and challenge them to guess the answers.

Name ______________________

▶ **Write a word from the box that best completes each sentence.**

talk	school	other	great	each	place

1. After ______________ Jan plays with her pets.

2. The birds ______________ together by chirping.

3. Jan gives an apple to ______________ bird.

4. The pups like to tackle each ______________.

5. Jan's house is a great ______________ for pets!

SCHOOL-HOME CONNECTION Ask your child to talk about what he or she likes to do after school. Encourage your child to draw a picture of the activity.

Name ______________________________

▶ **Circle the word that completes each sentence. Then write the word.**

1. Each of the twins has a ______________.

dimple
little
simple

2. Meg hid an ______________ in her napkin.

kettle
apple
chuckle

3. Do you like ______________ with your sandwich?

pickles
tickles
buckles

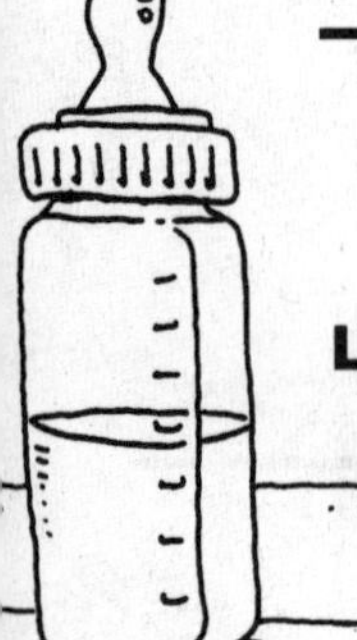

4. Gavin wants his ______________.

bubble
bottle
struggle

5. Gwen left a ______________ of milk.

candle
dimple
puddle

SCHOOL-HOME CONNECTION Ask your child to read the sentences aloud. Then make up silly tongue twisters using words with *-le*.

Name ______________________________

▶ **Finish each sentence. Add <u>er</u> or <u>est</u> to the word above the line**

small

1. A fox is ____________ than I am.

soft

2. A cat's fur is ____________ than a dog's.

fast

3. The ostrich is the ____________ animal.

smart

4. I am the ____________ of all.

SCHOOL-HOME CONNECTION Choose an object in your home. Ask your child to find something that is *bigger* than the object. Continue the game by having your child find other objects in your home that are bigger.

Name ______________________

▶ **Read the words. Then read the name of each group. Write each word in the group where it belongs.**

Words With oa	**Words With ow**
______	______
______	______
______	______

Words Without oa or ow

______	______
______	______

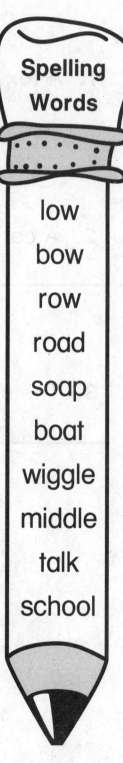

Spelling Words

low
bow
row
road
soap
boat
wiggle
middle
talk
school

SCHOOL-HOME CONNECTION Point to and read each Spelling Word with your child. Talk about what is the same and different about the words. Name more words with the long *o* sound.

Name ______________________________

▶ **Choose the correct column for each word in the box. Write the word under boat or crow.**

snow	coat	road	soap	bowl	bow

boat

crow

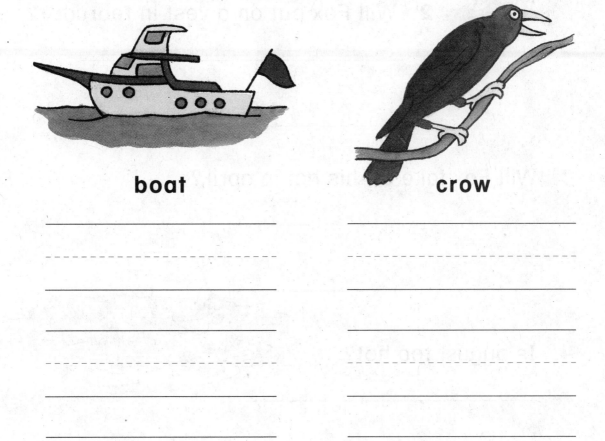

SCHOOL-HOME CONNECTION With your child, write a short poem with words that contain long vowel /ō/ spelled *oa* and *ow*.

Name ______________________

▶ **Read each sentence. Circle the name of the month. Then write the name correctly.**

1. Will it snow in january?

____

2. Will Fox put on a vest in february?

____

3. Will Fox take off his hat in april?

____

4. Is august too hot?

____

TRY THIS Write a sentence about the month you like best. Draw a picture to go with your sentence.

SCHOOL-HOME CONNECTION With your child, use a calendar to review the names of the months. Then help your child write the name of his or her birthday month.

Name ______________________

▶ **Write the word from the box that best completes each sentence.**

goat	grow	slow	mow

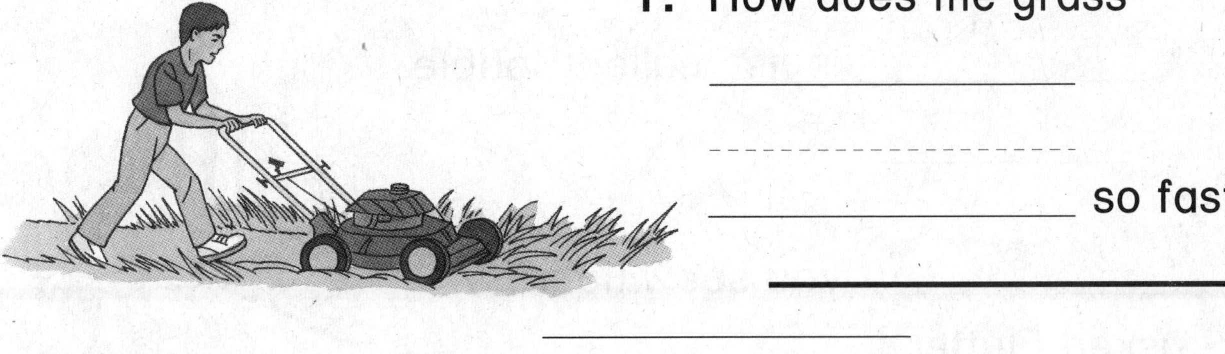

1. How does the grass ______________ so fast?

2. I wish it would ______________ down.

3. I don't like to ______________ the grass.

4. Would a ______________ eat my grass?

TRY THIS Write a sentence with the word boat. Draw a picture to go with your sentence.

SCHOOL-HOME CONNECTION Encourage your child to suggest words that have the same sound you hear in the middle of the word *boat*.

Name ______________________________

▶ **Write a word from the box to complete each sentence.**

door	kind	made	Who	Would

"__________ is it?" called Babble.

"__________ you see who it is?" asked Flutter.

Babble looked out the __________.

A box was on the mat. "Look! Two little coats."

"Who __________ these coats?" asked Babble.

Flutter read the tag. "How __________ of you to help us," it said.

SCHOOL-HOME CONNECTION Ask your child to read the words he or she wrote. Then have him or her use each word in a sentence.

Name ______________________________

▶ **Circle the word that names each picture. Then write the word.**

1. cot coat

2. top toad

3. box bowl

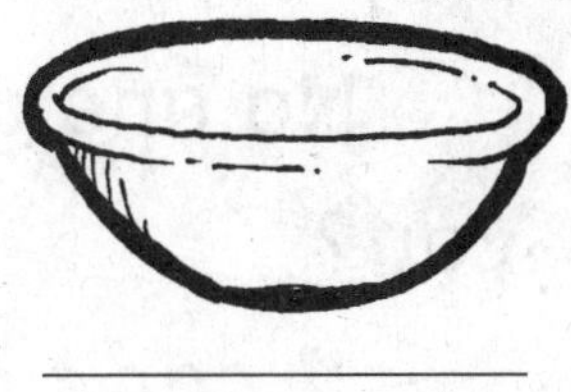

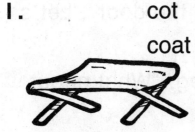

4. mop mow

5. rod road

6. Bob boat

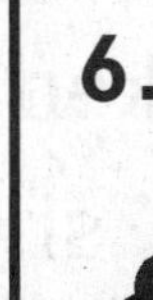

7. log load

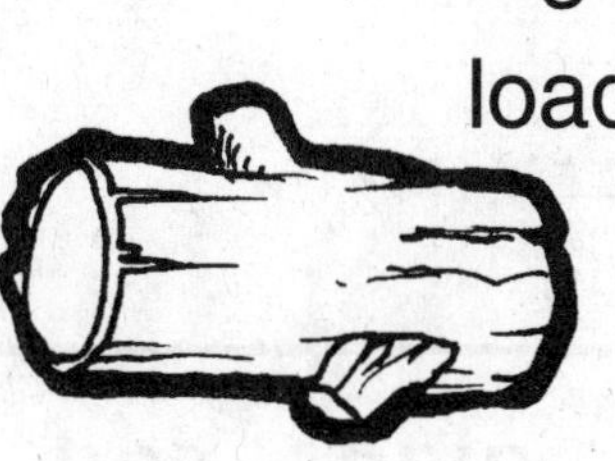

8. got goat

9. snow soap

SCHOOL-HOME CONNECTION Have your child read the words he or she wrote. Ask how your child knows whether to say the short *o* sound as in *on* or the long *o* sound as in *oak* and *own*.

Name ____________________

Read the story. Then circle and write the word that completes each sentence.

Meg grabbed her bat and ran to the door. "Let's play ball!" she called.

No one got up. "Jen?" asked Meg. "What about you?"

"I can't go out to play now," said Jen.

Meg looked at her dog. "Ruff, don't you want to play with me?"

Ruff did not get up.

Meg looked glum. "I'll just go out on my own," she said.

Meg **Max**

1. The main character is ________.

Meg **Jen**

2. Another character is ________.

glad **sad**

3. At the end of this story, Meg felt ________.

SCHOOL-HOME CONNECTION Have your child read the story aloud. Then ask what might happen if the story continued.

Name ______________________________

▶ **Put together the word and the word ending above each line. Write the new word to complete the sentence.**

play + ing

1. The friends are ______________ on the beach.

pick + ing

2. Dan is ______________ up shells.

help + ed

3. At first Carmen ______________ Dan.

run + s

4. Her dog ______________ in the sand.

SCHOOL-HOME CONNECTION With your child, talk about things you enjoy doing together. Try to use the words *played* and *playing* in your conversation.

Baby Chicks Hatch

1

The hen pecks for food.
She will not fly away.

3

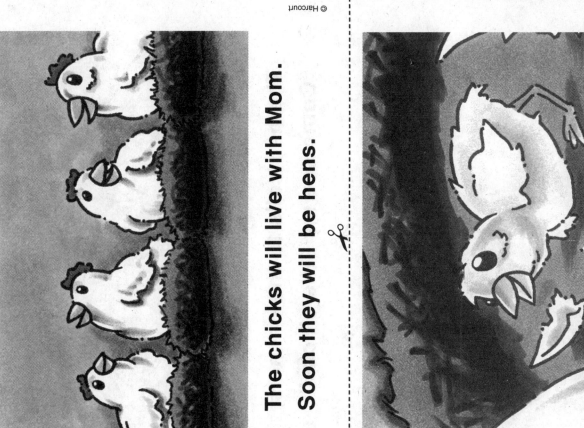

Chip, chip! A chick is out.
It hops around and smells the air.

6

The chicks will live with Mom.
Soon they will be hens.

8

Fold

Fold

"Cluck! Cluck!" says the hen.
2 Soon her eggs will hatch.

The hen calls to the animals,
"Come see my little chicks!" 7

Fold

She turns the eggs and
sits on them.
4 When will the eggs hatch?

Fold

Chip, chip! She checks the eggs.
An egg cracks! 5

Carmen sells all of her stars.
8 She likes to make and sell stars.

Carmen Sells Stars

1

Fold

"I make them," says Carmen.
6 "You can hang them in your house."

Fold

Carmen will sell stars there. 3

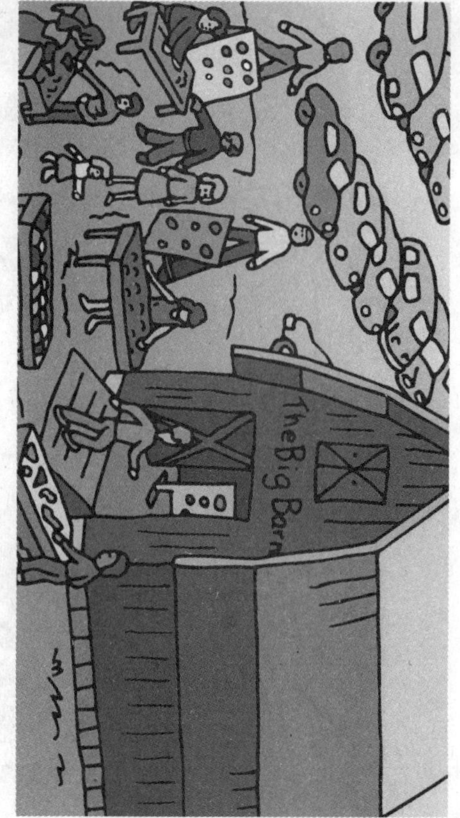

People from the city come for Craft Day.
The cars park at the big barn.

2

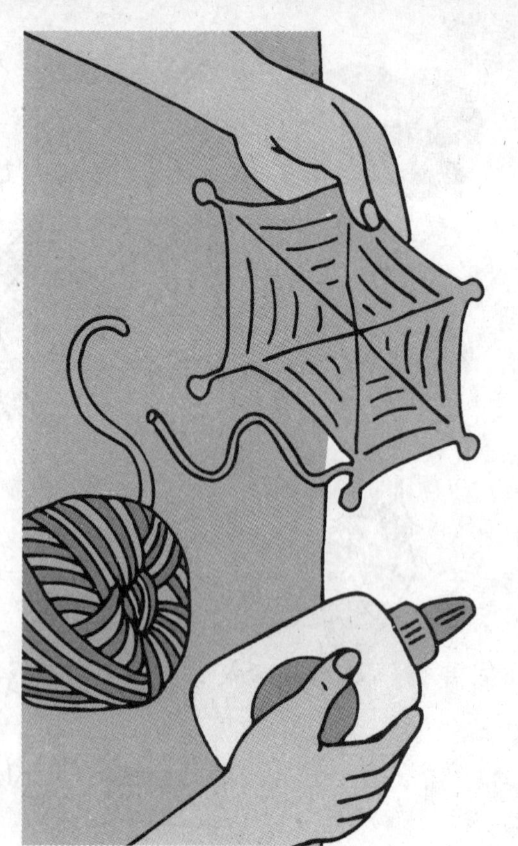

Sometimes the yarn slips off a star. Carmen fixes it.

4

Fold

People stop to take a look.
"We like your stars."

5

Fold

© Harcourt

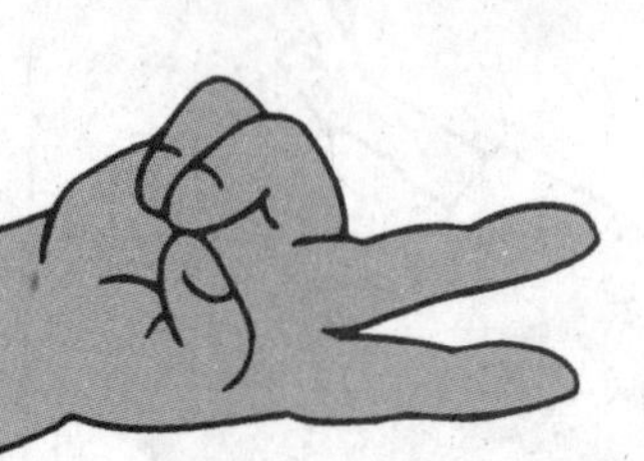

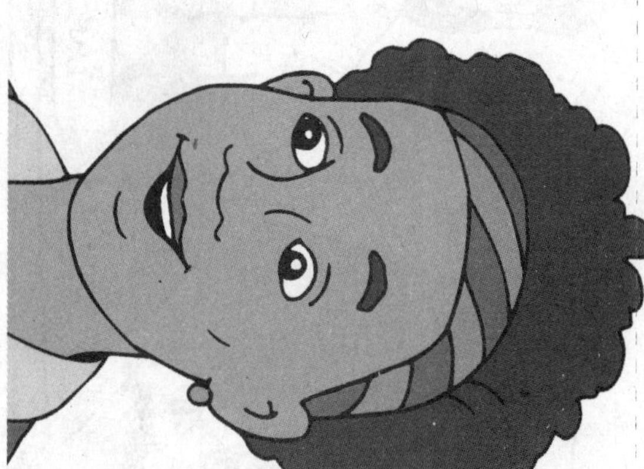

"I'll take two. I can give one to my friend Bart."

7

When did it happen?
8 I am writing about that night!

One Night

1

These ducks grew up in a house.
6 Quick! Let's get them out!

"Look, Dad! What's that?
It must want to come in." 3

Fold

Fold

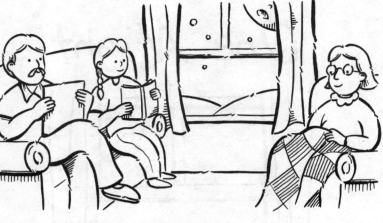

My family is sitting around.
Mom makes a quilt.
2 Dad and I read books.

Quack! Quack!
By ten they are all gone. 7

It's a bunch of ducks!
What's this all about?
4 Mom drops her quilt.

They are quacking and quacking!
It will take lots of work to get
them out! 5

Fold

Fold

Let's Play

1

Look at these jumps.
Can you jump like this?
Let's find out.

3

Oh, no! We were twirling in the dirt.
Now we are full of dirt.

6

We found a way to have some fun.
Why don't you try it?

8

Fold

Fold

Let's play. Follow me.
Jump this way.

2

Take four jumps.
Then turn and twirl.

4

We can twirl and swirl.
Jump this way and that.

5

My skirt is full of dirt.
My shirt is full of dirt.

7

Fold

Fold

Yes! We can play with
each other.It can
jump in puddles.
Hi, little pet.

8

Fold

A Jumping Pet

1

That is a great pet.
We could play
together.
But this pet
can't jump.

6

Fold

I've got a little
bug. It can
jump far.

3

I want a pet that can jump.

2

Here's a pet you'll like. It came from a wet place.

7

Fold

That's a nice little pet, but it's not what I want. I want a pet I can talk to.

4

Fold

What about a turtle? It's a great pet to bring to school.

5

Show what kinds of things were in the basket.

8

A Load of Stuff

1

Fold

The basket was harder and harder to lift. "Come on," said Toad. "We would do better up there."

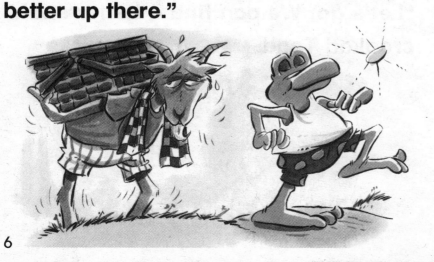

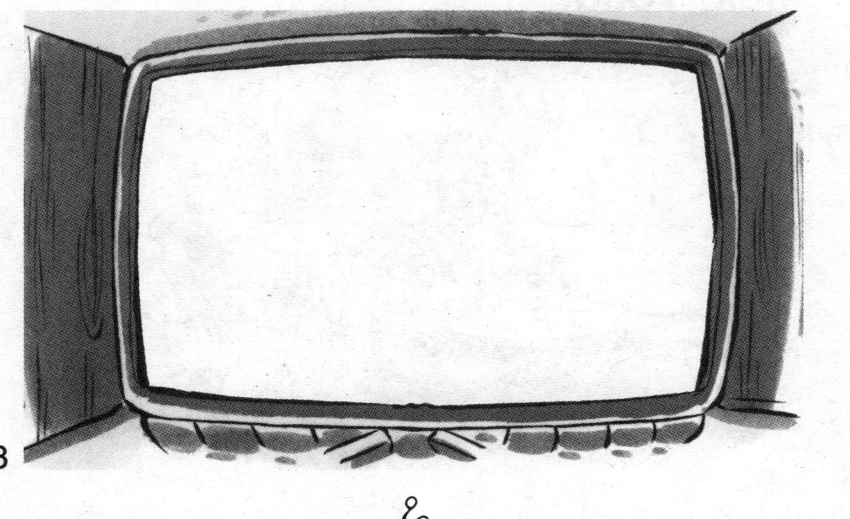

6

"What a load!" groaned Goat. "This must be the biggest lunch ever."

3

Fold

Goat met Toad at the door. "Let's go!" said Goat. "Let's go swimming!"

2

"I can't go any farther," said Goat. "This is the best spot. Let's eat," said Toad.

7

Fold

Goat and Toad walked down the road. The sun glowed. "I made a great lunch," said Toad.

4

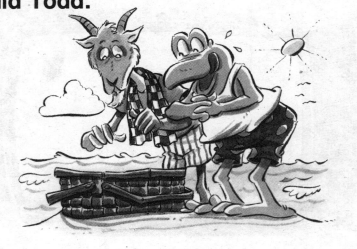

"Who loaded this basket?" moaned Goat.
"Let's go. We can find a better spot," croaked Toad.

5

Fold

Skills and Strategies Index

Skills and Strategies Index

SPELLING

VOCABULARY

End-of-Selection Tests

Grade 1

Name ______________________ Date __________

The Hat

Directions: You may wish to read the questions and answer choices to the children.

Directions: Fill in the circle by the correct answer.

Sample Dan ran ________.

- ◯ up
- ◯ down
- ◯ got

Vocabulary

1. Pam ran ________.

- ◯ down
- ◯ see
- ◯ got

Comprehension

2. Dan can see the ________.

- ◯ cat
- ◯ hat
- ◯ mat

Name ________________________ Date ________

The Hat

3. ________ can not get the hat.

- ◯ Sam
- ◯ Pam
- ◯ Dan

4. ________ got the hat for Pam.

- ◯ Pam
- ◯ Sam
- ◯ Dan

Name ______________________________ Date __________

The Hat

Directions: Draw or write the answer to the question.

5. What is this story about?

Name ______________________ Date __________

Sam and the Bag

Directions: Fill in the circle by the correct answer.

Sample Max ran ________ the bag.

◯ and

◯ up

◯ in

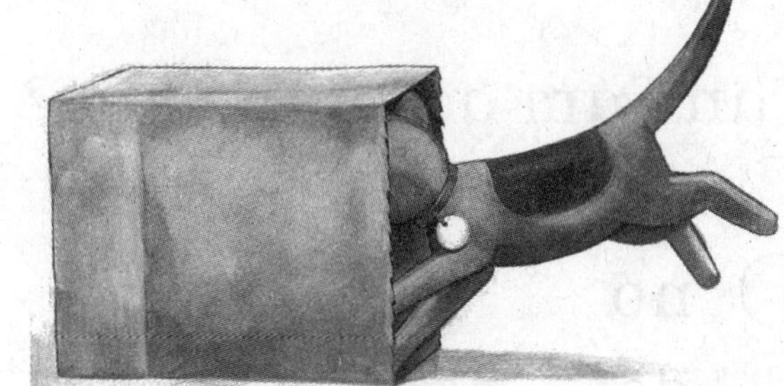

Vocabulary

1. Max ________ Hap are in the bag.

◯ and

◯ on

◯ yes

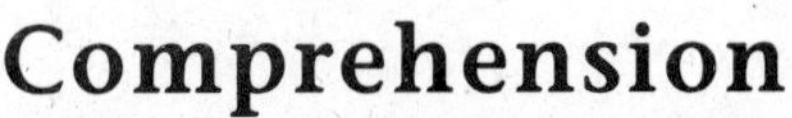

Comprehension

2. Sam ran ________.

◯ down the bag

◯ up the bag

◯ in the bag

Name ______________________ Date __________

Sam and the Bag

3. _______ is in the bag.

- ◯ Hap
- ◯ Max
- ◯ Sam

4. Can Sam go in the bag?

- ◯ yes
- ◯ no
- ◯ do

Name ______________________ Date __________

Sam and the Bag

Directions: Draw or write the answer to the question.

5. What happened when Sam got in the bag?

Name ______________________ Date ________

Ants

Directions: Fill in the circle by the correct answer.

Sample The ant can ________.

- ◯ make
- ◯ they
- ◯ walk

Vocabulary

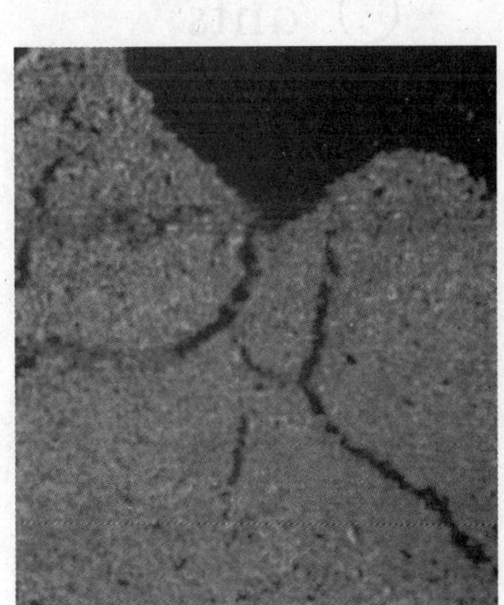

1. Look at the ants.
________ make big homes.

- ◯ They
- ◯ Make
- ◯ Down

Comprehension

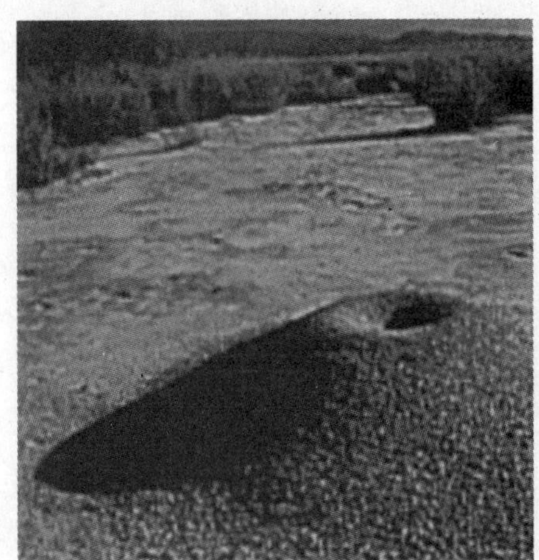

2. Where do ants make homes?

- ◯ in the bag
- ◯ in the can
- ◯ in the hill

Name ______________________________ Date __________

Ants

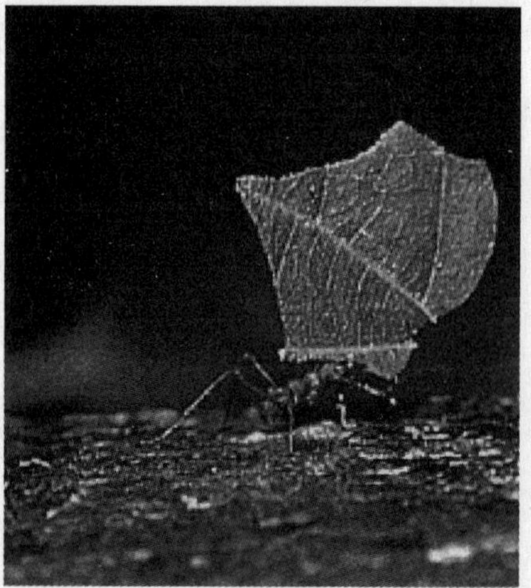

3. What can the ants do?

- ◯ They can lift.
- ◯ They can dig.
- ◯ They get in the bag.

4. This story is about _______.

- ◯ cats
- ◯ hats
- ◯ ants

Name ______________________ Date __________

Ants

Directions: Draw or write the answer to the question.

5. What is one thing you can do like an ant?

Name ______________________ Date ______

Jack and Rick

Directions: Fill in the circle by the correct answer.

Sample Jack wants to ________ with Rick.

◯ help

◯ play

◯ now

Vocabulary

1. Jack can ________ Rick.

◯ help

◯ two

◯ walk

Comprehension

2. Can Jack pick up the log?

◯ No! It is too little.

◯ No! It is too big.

◯ Yes! It is a big rope.

Name ________________________________ Date __________

Jack and Rick

3. Rick can pass a ________ to Jack.

◯ rope
◯ log
◯ bag

4. Do Rick and Jack lift the log?

◯ no
◯ yes
◯ now

Name ______________________ Date __________

Jack and Rick

Directions: Draw or write the end to the sentence.

5. Rick walks on the log and he ________.

Name ____________________ Date ________

Todd's Box

Directions: Fill in the circle by the correct answer.

Sample ________ dig now, Todd.

- ◯ So
- ◯ Don't
- ◯ Walk

Vocabulary

1. Todd has a box ________ surprises.

- ◯ so
- ◯ of
- ◯ in

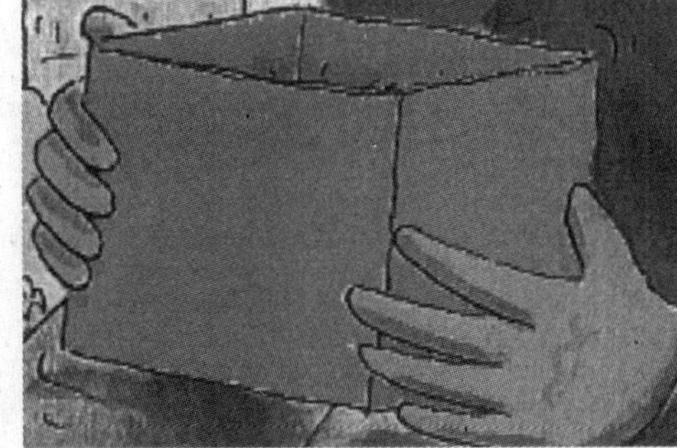

Comprehension

2. Todd likes to ________ in the sand.

- ◯ dig
- ◯ do
- ◯ help

Name ______________________________ Date __________

Todd's Box

3. Todd is on the ________.

◯ rope
◯ log
◯ rocks

4. Todd sees a ________.

◯ pond
◯ log
◯ bag

Name ______________________________ Date __________

Todd's Box

Directions: Draw or write the end to the sentence.

5. Todd and Mom go home on the ________.

Name ______________________ Date __________

All That Corn

Directions: Fill in the circle by the correct answer.

Sample ________ is the corn?

◯ Want
◯ Very
◯ Where

Vocabulary

1. We can ________ corn in a store.

◯ here
◯ buy
◯ that

Comprehension

2. That corn is very ________.

◯ little
◯ very
◯ tall

Name ______________________________ Date __________

All That Corn

3. They _______ the corn.
   - ◯ pick
   - ◯ can
   - ◯ look

4. Corn can go in _______.
   - ◯ ropes and cans
   - ◯ plays and bags
   - ◯ cans and bags

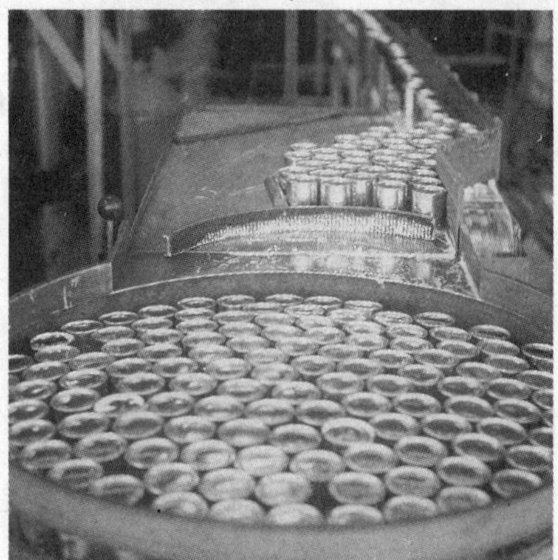

Name ______________________________ Date __________

All That Corn

Directions: Draw or write the answer to the question.

5. What do you get when you pop corn?

Name ______________________ Date ________

Dan's Pet

Directions: Fill in the circle by the correct answer.

Sample The baby chick ________ soft in Dan's hands.

- ○ where
- ○ was
- ○ walk

Vocabulary

1. Mom and I walk every ________.

- ○ my
- ○ with
- ○ day

2. Dan ________, "Look at the little hen."

- ○ said
- ○ help
- ○ play

3. Rick will help ________.

- ○ at
- ○ have
- ○ her

Name ______________________ Date ________

Dan's Pet

4. Will Pat play ______ Sam and Pam?
   - ◯ want
   - ◯ with
   - ◯ what

5. They fed the hens ______ day.
   - ◯ little
   - ◯ every
   - ◯ very

Comprehension

6. Dan's pet is a ______.
   - ◯ cat
   - ◯ chick
   - ◯ hen

7. Dan ______ with the hens and the chicks.
   - ◯ makes
   - ◯ helps
   - ◯ looks

8. Dan calls his pet ______.
   - ◯ Jen
   - ◯ Pam
   - ◯ Jack

Name ______________________ Date __________

Dan's Pet

9. Jen got very ______.

- ◯ down
- ◯ yes
- ◯ big

Directions: Draw or write the answer to the question.

10. What surprise did Dan get?

Name ______________________________ Date ________

Boots for Beth

Directions: Fill in the circle by the correct answer.

Sample He can ________ on his boots.

- ○ want
- ○ look
- ○ put

Vocabulary

1. My ________ are here.

- ○ friends
- ○ and
- ○ with

2. I have ________ boots.

- ○ walk
- ○ use
- ○ new

3. Here is Beth. ________ is sad.

- ○ He
- ○ She
- ○ Her

Name ______________________ Date __________

Boots for Beth

4. Pam ________ make a hat.

- ◯ could
- ◯ buy
- ◯ here

5. Jack wants to ________ the rope.

- ◯ don't
- ◯ use
- ◯ help

Comprehension

6. Beth can not use her red boots. They don't ________.

- ◯ fit
- ◯ get
- ◯ look

7. Ned's boots are too ________ for Beth.

- ◯ small
- ◯ big
- ◯ soft

8. Meg's boots are too ________ for Beth.

- ◯ tall
- ◯ little
- ◯ big

Name ______________________________ Date __________

Boots for Beth

9. Beth's friends felt ________ for Beth.

- ◯ little
- ◯ bad
- ◯ red

Directions: Draw or write the answer to the question.

10. What do the friends do for Beth?

Name ______________________ Date ________

Space Pup

Directions: Fill in the circle by the correct answer.

Sample ________ is a big man.

- ○ Help
- ○ He
- ○ Yes

Vocabulary

1. Dan ________ a baby chick to Pam.

- ○ gives
- ○ was
- ○ could

2. My friends don't play at ________.

- ○ what
- ○ night
- ○ little

3. ________ can Jen have the surprises?

- ○ Want
- ○ What
- ○ When

Name ______________________ Date __________

Space Pup

4. All the ________ are here.

◯ your
◯ people
◯ says

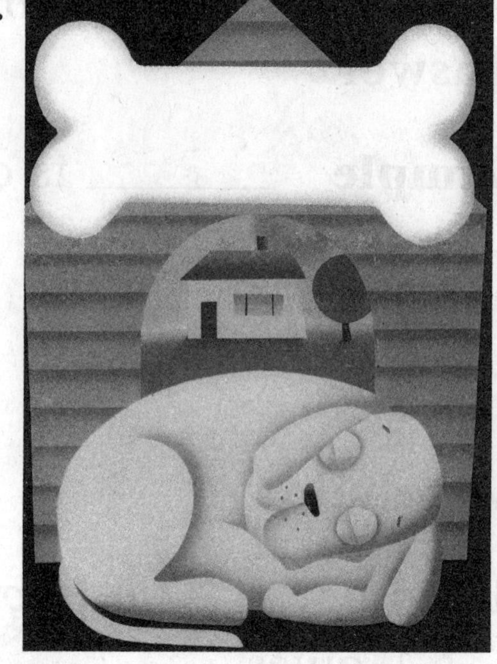

5. The pet is ________.

◯ out
◯ are
◯ help

Comprehension

6. What is Gus?

◯ a people pup
◯ a space pup
◯ a help pup

7. When does Gus rest?

◯ day
◯ night
◯ now

8. The bus is ________ the mud.

◯ out of
◯ in
◯ up to

9. What does Space Pup do with the rope?

- ◯ gets the bus out of the mud
- ◯ gets the people
- ◯ hands it to the man

Directions: Draw or write the answer to the question.

10. What is the story about?

Name ______________________ Date ________

Where Do Frogs Come From?

Directions: Fill in the circle by the correct answer.

Sample The big bag is ________ Pam.

- ◯ now
- ◯ hen
- ◯ from

Vocabulary

1. The ________ frogs are here.

- ◯ two
- ◯ one
- ◯ every

2. The tadpole ________ big.

- ◯ wants
- ◯ grows
- ◯ gone

3. The fish likes to ________ plants.

- ◯ buy
- ◯ help
- ◯ eat

Name ______________________ Date ________

Where Do Frogs Come From?

4. They have _______ home.

- ◯ gone
- ◯ like
- ◯ eat

5. Do you have one _______ two eggs?

- ◯ and
- ◯ or
- ◯ up

Comprehension

6. Tadpoles come from _______.

- ◯ eggs
- ◯ hens
- ◯ chicks

7. A tadpole has _______.

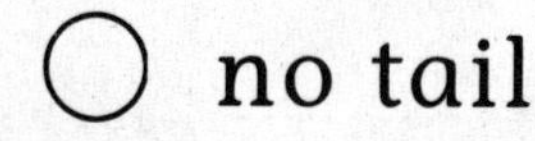

- ◯ no tail
- ◯ a long tail
- ◯ two legs

8. A frog has no tail. So it can _______.

- ◯ swim
- ◯ eat
- ◯ hop

Name ______________________________ Date __________

Where Do Frogs Come From?

9. A frog eats ________.

- ◯ fish
- ◯ corn
- ◯ bugs

Directions: Draw or write the answer to the question.

10. How do eggs grow to be frogs?

Name ______________________ Date ________

Try Your Best

Directions: Fill in the circle by the correct answer.

Sample Pam is ________ at sports.

- ○ good
- ○ up
- ○ down

Vocabulary

1. It is ________ to go home now.

- ○ that
- ○ time
- ○ night

2. We ________ to play our best.

- ○ try
- ○ saw
- ○ grow

3. We ________ two frogs.

- ○ saw
- ○ says
- ○ was

Name ______________________ Date __________

Try Your Best

4. Will you play on ______ team?

- ◯ our
- ◯ are
- ◯ so

5. Do you have to ______ home at two?

- ◯ eat
- ◯ be
- ◯ grow

Comprehension

6. What day is it?

- ◯ Sports Day
- ◯ Pet Day
- ◯ Hat Day

7. ______ likes to play sports.

- ◯ Ann
- ◯ Jan
- ◯ Mr. York

8. The kick Ann made helped the team ______.

- ◯ run
- ◯ race
- ◯ score

Name ______________________ Date ________

Try Your Best

9. Mort wants ________ to be on the team.

- ◯ Mr. York
- ◯ Ann
- ◯ Jan

Directions: Draw or write the end to the sentence.

10. When Mr. York runs in the race, he sees a ________.

Name ________________________________ Date ________

Fun with Fish

Directions: Fill in the circle by the correct answer.

Sample ________ fish eat plants.

- ○ Said
- ○ Some
- ○ Saw

Vocabulary

1. The rockfish likes to ________ in the rocks.

- ○ here
- ○ hide
- ○ how

2. The clown fish looks ________.

- ○ funny
- ○ from
- ○ food

3. The little fish swims ________ from the big fish.

- ○ to
- ○ very
- ○ away

Name ______________________ Date __________

Fun with Fish

4. ________ people like to swim with the fish.

- ◯ Many
- ◯ Make
- ◯ Me

5. Fish use ________ tails to help them swim.

- ◯ they
- ◯ their
- ◯ that

Comprehension

6. What do some big fish eat?

- ◯ small fish
- ◯ sand
- ◯ rocks

7. Fish hide in ________.

- ◯ plants and fish
- ◯ sand and plants
- ◯ sand and rods

8. One fish looks mad.
That fish has ________ teeth.

- ◯ little
- ◯ no
- ◯ big

Name ______________________ Date __________

Fun with Fish

9. The fish that is a friend eats ______.

- ◯ food off the friend's skin
- ◯ the friend's food
- ◯ rocks

Directions: Draw or write the answer to the question.

10. What fish did you like best?

Name ______________________ Date ________

I Am a Butterfly

Directions: Fill in the circle by the correct answer.

Sample Some ________ run and hop.

- ○ corn
- ○ animals
- ○ fish

Vocabulary

1. Some animals ________ in nests.

- ○ like
- ○ look
- ○ live

2. A butterfly can ________.

- ○ fly
- ○ for
- ○ frog

3. We will be home ________.

- ○ some
- ○ away
- ○ soon

Name ________________________ Date ________

I Am a Butterfly

4. Many frogs and bugs live ________ here.

- ◯ away
- ◯ around
- ◯ from

5. The butterfly can fly up in the ________.

- ◯ air
- ◯ like
- ◯ am

Comprehension

6. The butterfly egg sits on a ________.

- ◯ rock
- ◯ web
- ◯ plant

7. The butterfly egg hatches into a ________.

- ◯ caterpillar
- ◯ frog
- ◯ slug

8. A caterpillar ________ plants.

- ◯ eats
- ◯ works
- ◯ plays

9. How many legs does an insect have?

- ◯ two
- ◯ four
- ◯ six

Directions: Draw or write the answer to the question.

10. How do wings help a butterfly?

Name ______________________ Date ________

Did You See Chip?

Directions: Fill in the circle by the correct answer.

Sample My friend lives in a big ________.

- ○ food
- ○ could
- ○ city

Vocabulary

1. I can see my ________ from here.

- ○ house
- ○ day
- ○ how

2. You can ________ the food to the animals now.

- ○ turns
- ○ take
- ○ make

3. It is ________ fun to play tag.

- ○ soon
- ○ around
- ○ sometimes

Name ______________________ Date ________

4. That man is ________ Day.

- ○ Miss
- ○ Mr.
- ○ so

5. We walk ________ every day.

- ○ there
- ○ they
- ○ from

Comprehension

6. Chip wants to go ________.

- ○ to the park
- ○ for a walk
- ○ for a hot dog

7. Kim wishes her friends lived by her ________.

- ○ on the farm
- ○ in the city
- ○ in the new house

8. They want to catch Chip so he will not ________.

- ○ take a nap
- ○ get lost
- ○ go to the farm

Name ______________________ Date ________

9. Where do they catch up with Chip?

- ◯ at home
- ◯ at the park
- ◯ by the hot dog cart

Directions: Draw or write the answer to the question.

10. Who helped Kim and her dad look for Chip?

Name ______________________ Date ________

Tomás Rivera

Directions: Fill in the circle by the correct answer.

Sample Tomás likes to read ________.

- ○ air
- ○ about
- ○ books

Vocabulary

1. Do you have a big ________?

- ○ many
- ○ family
- ○ work

2. The corn ________ very tall.

- ○ great
- ○ go
- ○ grew

3. Do you like ________ stories?

- ○ writing
- ○ about
- ○ want

4. They ________ on a farm picking crops.

- ◯ take
- ◯ work
- ◯ sometimes

5. Bill can walk to the library ________ himself.

- ◯ so
- ◯ by
- ◯ be

Comprehension

6. Tomás was born in ________.

- ◯ Texas
- ◯ the city
- ◯ the library

7. Tomás and his family ________.

- ◯ work at the library
- ◯ pick crops
- ◯ fish every day

8. ________ tells Tomás the best stories.

- ◯ Mother
- ◯ Father
- ◯ Grandpa

Name ______________________________ Date __________

Tomás Rivera

9. What will help Tomás think of stories by himself?

- ◯ reading all he can
- ◯ walking fast
- ◯ reading about bugs

Directions: Draw or write the answer to the question.

10. Where can Tomás get books to read?

Name ______________________ Date ________

On the Way to the Pond

Directions: Fill in the circle by the correct answer.

Sample Look at the ________ clowns.

○ four
○ about
○ some

Vocabulary

1. Pat ________ the big pond.

○ full
○ found
○ fun

2. "Walk this ________," said the teacher.

○ what
○ way
○ play

3. The cats ________ in the house.

○ were
○ where
○ want

Name ______________________________ Date __________

On the Way to the Pond

4. Pam can ________ you to the store.

- ◯ friends
- ◯ full
- ◯ follow

5. ________ are my books.

- ◯ About
- ◯ The
- ◯ These

Comprehension

6. Herbert packs a ________.

- ◯ picnic basket
- ◯ book bag
- ◯ funny hat

7. Two of the important things Tess brings are a ________.

- ◯ basket and a hat
- ◯ fan and an umbrella
- ◯ rope and a fish

8. It was so hot Herbert felt ________.

- ◯ little
- ◯ tall
- ◯ sick

Name ______________________________ Date ________

On the Way to the Pond

9. On the way back to Herbert, Tess ________.

- ◯ can not find the way
- ◯ plays and runs
- ◯ eats the lunch

Directions: Draw or write the answer to the question.

10. To get back to Herbert at the pond, Tess follows ________.

Name ____________________ Date ________

Friends Forever

Directions: Fill in the circle by the correct answer.

Sample I like to ________ to my friends.

- ○ play
- ○ were
- ○ talk

Vocabulary

1. My friend and I like to be ________.

- ○ together
- ○ worker
- ○ these

2. Do you walk to ________?

- ○ soon
- ○ school
- ○ great

3. ________ of us have two fish.

- ○ Were
- ○ Jump
- ○ Each

Name ______________________ Date ________

4. This is a nice ______.
   - ◯ place
   - ◯ funny
   - ◯ there

5. Where is the ______ book?
   - ◯ hide
   - ◯ other
   - ◯ many

Comprehension

6. The friends like to ______ together.
   - ◯ hunt for shells
   - ◯ eat rocks
   - ◯ be sad

7. On a team, friends can ______.
   - ◯ go pop
   - ◯ kick the ball
   - ◯ act silly

8. The dog is pals with the ______.
   - ◯ pig
   - ◯ butterfly
   - ◯ cat

Name ______________________ Date ________

Friends Forever

9. Where is a good place to find a friend?

- ○ in the library
- ○ fishing
- ○ at school

Directions: Draw or write the answer to the question.

10. What are some things you can share with your friends at school?

Name ______________________ Date __________

Directions: Fill in the circle by the correct answer.

Sample Long ago there was a fox ________ was friends with a stork.

- ◯ two
- ◯ here
- ◯ who

Vocabulary

1. Dad ________ very good soup for lunch.

- ◯ made
- ◯ follow
- ◯ grew

2. The ________ of my house is red.

- ◯ there
- ◯ door
- ◯ place

3. Fox asked Stork, "________ you like some soup?"

- ◯ Now
- ◯ Writing
- ◯ Would

4. Are you ________ to your friends?

- ◯ kind
- ◯ about
- ◯ find

Comprehension

5. Fox lives in a ________ .

- ◯ food
- ◯ forest
- ◯ house

6. Fox likes to play________ his friends.

- ◯ games with
- ◯ school with
- ◯ tricks on

7. Fox serves the soup to Stork in a ________ .

- ◯ beautiful cup
- ◯ tall jar
- ◯ flat dish

8. Stork could not get the soup, but Stork did not ________ .

- ◯ complain
- ◯ go hungry
- ◯ like the soup

Name ______________________ Date ________

The Fox and the Stork

9. Fox _______ when Stork played a trick on him.

- ◯ liked it
- ◯ did not like it
- ◯ got mad

Directions: Complete the sentence by drawing or writing the answer.

10. Stork tricks Fox by _______.